*Queen Victoria
in Switzerland*

Queen Victoria in Switzerland

PETER ARENGO-JONES

ROBERT HALE · LONDON

© Peter Arengo-Jones 1995
First published in Great Britain 1995

ISBN 0 7090 5365 7

Robert Hale Limited
Clerkenwell House
Clerkenwell Green
London EC1R 0HT

The right of Peter Arengo-Jones to be identified as
author of this work has been asserted by him
in accordance with the Copyright, Designs and
Patents Act 1988.

2 4 6 8 10 9 7 5 3 1

Photoset in North Wales by
Derek Doyle & Associates, Mold, Clwyd.
Printed in Hong Kong by
Bookbuilders Ltd.

Contents

Acknowledgements — 7
Glossary of Familiar Names — 8
Author's Note — 11

PART ONE

1. Settled Desolation — 15
2. Incognita — 36

PART TWO

3. Haven — 63
4. Frustration — 78
5. 'Purer, Lighter Mountain Air' — 85
6. Exploration — 101
7. Incognita – the Acid Test — 116
8. The Final Week — 120

PART THREE

9. Aftermath — 139
10. Echo in Switzerland — 151

References — 154
Illustration Sources — 158
Index — 159

Acknowledgements

Material from the Royal Library and Archives at Windsor (Queen Victoria's Journal and correspondence, watercolours and sketches by her and Princess Louise, photographs) is published by gracious permission of Her Majesty the Queen.

The author is grateful for generous help and guidance given by: Mr Oliver Everett, Librarian and Assistant Keeper of the Archives at Windsor and his predecessor Sir Robin Mackworth-Young; The Hon. Mrs Roberts, Curator of the Print Room; Lady de Bellaigue, Registrar of the Royal Archives; Miss G. Campling, Head of Photographic Services; Miss F. Dimond, Curator of the Royal Photograph Collection and Lt.-Col. Seymour Gilbart-Denham, Crown Equerry, the Royal Mews and their staffs.

Further, the author wishes to thank Moritz, Landgraf von Hessen and the Hessische Hausstiftung at the Fasanerie, Fulda (where Frau Nicolette Luthmer was particularly helpful) for permission to quote from Queen Victoria's letters to her daughter Victoria, Princess Royal of Prussia.

Grateful acknowledgement is also made to the Earl of Derby for permission to use material from the Papers of the 15th Earl of Derby, as well as to the Liverpool Record Office, Liverpool Libraries and Information Services where they are housed.

The author would like to thank Dr J.M. Fewster, Senior Assistant Keeper of Archives and Special Collections at the University of Durham Library for his help with the papers of General Charles Grey.

Crown copyright material held in the Public Record Office is reproduced with the permission of the Controller of Her Majesty's Stationery Office.

For use of material from the Hughenden Papers acknowledgement is made to the Bodleian Library, Oxford which holds the Disraeli manuscripts from Hughenden Manor on permanent deposit from the National Trust.

Illustrations from the graphical collection at the Zentralbibliothek Luzern are reproduced here by permission of the Director, Dr A. Schacher. The author is grateful to him and his staff for their generosity and patient help.

Finally, the author is greatly indebted to the many people without whose help, support and encouragement all along this book would not have been possible.

Glossary of Familiar Names

Affie	Prince Alfred, Duke of Edinburgh, Queen Victoria's 2nd son
Baby	Princess Beatrice, Queen Victoria's youngest daughter
Bids	Sir Thomas Biddulph, Keeper of Her Majesty's Privy Purse
Janie	Jane, Marchioness of Ely, Lady of the Bedchamber

For Evelyn

Author's Note

Throughout this text there are curious spellings as well as variations in the spelling of the same word, place or name. The originator's spelling has usually been retained, with a footnote in some instances to avoid confusion (e.g. Queen Victoria's 'Alten' instead of 'Olten'). The originator's abbreviations have also been retained, e.g. 'wd' for 'would', 'shd' for 'should', 'Ly' for 'Lady', 'Ld' for 'Lord'.

Queen Victoria's Journal as we have it is a transcript made by her youngest daughter, Princess Beatrice. Queen Victoria had instructed that the Journal should be burned after her death. Before doing so, the Princess copied a good proportion of the text. But we have no means of knowing how much is omitted.

In this book quotations and extracts from the Journal are in italics.

PART
One

1 Settled Desolation

On 31 August 1868 Queen Victoria, thinly disguised as 'The Countess of Kent', sat on the grass of a Swiss Alpine meadow on her way down from a 7,000 ft mountain, enjoying her afternoon tea[1] – her attendants having made light work of obstacles such as the non-availability of a kettle and the near-impossibility of finding water nearby.

This is the stuff of which British travellers in the nineteenth century were made. This is the spirit behind the peaceful conquest of Switzerland by the British. All over the country the Queen's subjects were doing similar things, some more strenuously and adventurously, some more sedately. But very few will have had to go to such lengths as their Queen to get away to Switzerland. For her, this holiday was the culmination of years of planning, hoping and plotting.

For six years Queen Victoria had been shrouding herself in seclusion. In 1868 she was in the seventh year of mourning for Prince Albert, the Prince Consort, whose death in 1861 had robbed her life of its light. She was forty-nine, diminutive in height and of late rotund, the mother of nine children and the sovereign of a quarter of the world's population. It was said that she had not smiled since the bereavement that had so shattered her. Albert had more than shared the burden of her responsibilities. Deprived of his counsel and protection she felt lost and insecure, convinced that she was not up to the task of being Queen by herself. She dreaded appearing in public. Although she gritted her teeth and performed her royal duties whenever absolutely necessary, each time the effort was

'He protected me, He comforted and encouraged me.'
Queen Victoria with Prince Albert at Buckingham Palace, 1854

agonising. She appeared stiff and aloof, whereas by nature she was the opposite.

> ... her simple and formidable character was compounded of a few basic and universal elements. By nature she was almost all the things that the typical woman is alleged to be by those who have the temerity to generalize on the subject; instinctive, personal, unintellectual, partizan, interested in detail, viewing things in the concrete rather than the abstract, and with a profound natural reverence for the secure and the respectable. With these common qualities of her sex, the Queen possessed also those of her age ... though regal, she was not aristocratic as the English understand the term. The healthy, homely German blood which coursed through her veins had imparted a commonplace, even a bourgeois tinge to her taste. But if her nature was normal, her character was not. It was too abnormally high-powered for one thing. Her enjoyments were more rapturous than the average girl's, her sentimentality more unbridled, her interest in detail more inexhaustible, her partizanship more violent, her innocence more dewy. Some strain in her – once again it may have come from Germany – had endowed her with an extravagant force of temperament; so that the ordinary in her was magnified to a degree where it became extraordinary ... To this startling fervour of feeling she added a startling simplicity of vision.[2]

This character sketch by David Cecil is in marked contrast to the traditional but woefully over-simplified perception of Queen Victoria as the epitome of the Victorian: unamused, straitlaced, prudish. Published in 1954, it was foreshadowed by others, even Lytton Strachey's more than a quarter of a century earlier, and has been followed by many a biography presenting a more differentiated picture of her personality. But the image of the severe Queen, withdrawn and in solemn black, is so deeply embedded as to have survived to this day, even now overlaying our appreciation of the sunnier and spontaneous side of the Queen's personality that struggled through as she emerged from the depths of mourning and acquired self-confidence as a monarch in her own right.

Queen Victoria's Swiss holiday in 1868 helped her along this road, but she had a long way to come. The death of Prince Albert had been such a devastating blow that she took years to come out of shock, and the rest of her life – spent more or less in mourning – trying to come to terms with her loss, although by the 1870s she had achieved a resigned balance. But during the 1860s her insistence on seclusion became a serious national problem, even raising the question of her abdication.

Her family and her courtiers did what they could, notably her then still unofficial Private Secretary, General Grey, to whom she wrote in 1863 (in the customary third person):

> ... she cannot deny that <u>he</u> is her <u>main</u> support & when <u>he</u> is away, she always

General Grey playing a salmon in the Dee

feels <u>additionally anxious</u>. She is <u>not</u> worrying herself just now, & is calmer; but her constant & ever increasing grief – added to a terribly nervous temperament by nature (which her precious Husband knew but too well & often had to suffer from she fears, but wh <u>he naturally</u> cld <u>calm</u> as she cld at any moment of the day & night pour out <u>all</u> to him) – prevents her taking <u>anything calmly</u>.[3]

So, with her ever-present need for a father-figure and male shoulder to lean on, it was not surprising that she turned to General Grey to confide in and discuss travel plans. For example, she told him of her intention of spending three weeks in 1863 at Coburg, Prince Albert's family seat in Germany (in what used to be the province of Saxe-Coburg-Gotha) and thus a place with special associations for the Queen. She wrote to General Grey that she felt the need to go there:

… as she feels it <u>almost a duty</u> to do something for her <u>wretched health</u> & nerves, to prevent further increase of depression & exhaustion.

God knows her <u>own</u> inclination would be to do <u>nothing</u> for her health, as <u>her</u> only wish is to see her <u>life end soon</u>, but she feels that <u>if</u> she is to go on, <u>she must</u> change the <u>scene</u> completely sometimes – (if it does not affect, & she hopes it does <u>not</u>, her duties) – consequently – going to Balmoral for a fortnight or 3 weeks in the <u>Spring</u> & to <u>Coburg</u> (<u>Coburg only</u>) in the <u>Summer</u> for <u>3 weeks</u> – (besides visiting her dear Uncle at Brussels; which is a duty) & quite necessary.

Her Beloved Angel wld _not_ – if He were asked & saw _how_ weak & bowed to the earth with anguish & desolation she is – ever, ever _encreasing_ – object to her making these _additional moves_.4

Those around the Queen knew perfectly well where the real problem lay. That summer Grey wrote from Coburg to a trusted Court official, Sir Charles Phipps, Keeper of the Privy Purse:

I have since had a long conversation with Princess Alice,* who says the Queen _is_ very well. She got through her luncheon of 18 to the Emperor of Austria perfectly, talked a great deal – & was interested – running to the window & to see him drive away. Princess Alice also says that the Queen owned to her she was afraid of getting too well – as if it was a crime & that she _feared_ to begin to like riding on her Scotch poney &c&c. She is so nice & touching in her manner that it is difficult to find the heart to urge her to anything she does not like – but after the next anniversary, we must all try, _gently_, to get her to resume her old habits.5

'… _this feeling of settled desolation._'
Queen Victoria to Crown Princess Victoria, 3 September 1867

---

* Queen Victoria's second daughter, the future Grand Duchess of Hesse-Darmstadt.

This was easier said than done. It was to take a long time.

She did travel. But for some years she never ventured beyond the familiar and comforting round of her own residences and those of her close family abroad. One of these was the summer house Rosenau near Coburg, in which Prince Albert had been born. Yet the Rosenau, peaceful though it was, had a drawback. There were always too many people around.

It was when staying there in August 1865, in search of peace and quiet, that a new idea started to crystallize, took hold of her and did not let go until she had put it into practice three years later.

She immediately put the idea to General Grey in a memo.

August 28 1865
The Queen does feel that she <u>must</u> try some day to spend <u>4</u> weeks in some <u>completely quiet</u> spot in Switzerland where she can refuse <u>all</u> visitors and have <u>complete</u> quiet. The first week here she <u>felt</u> the benefit of the quiet; but since last Tuesday she has not had one day's repose and since Monday has been quite overwhelmed by the number of visitors and relations so that she regrets she did not decide to stay here 3 or 4 days longer to recruit herself before starting on the journey. Seriously, she thinks that if she is alive (and alas! she must live on) <u>next year</u> she must try and do something to get a little <u>complete</u> rest for she feels that <u>her nerves</u> and her <u>strength</u> are getting <u>more</u> and <u>more exhausted and worn</u>. She has been talking to Kanné* and also to Major Elphinstone† but she wished the General would also speak to them, for what the Queen <u>wants</u> is to choose some <u>very retired spot</u> in a fine part of Switzerland which she could get at without too long a journey; she does <u>not</u> wish to <u>travel about</u> in <u>Switzerland</u> or to go and <u>see</u> anything very fatiguing for her strength and nerves would not stand that. She would go with a reduced party, take no horses but perhaps <u>2</u> ponies for herself to ride and <u>live as simply</u> and in as retired a way as possible. General Grey understands this from his knowledge of her Highland expeditions and she fears Kanné hardly does. Then he says that the Queen would have to sleep at Darmstadt and then go still <u>two nights</u> resting one day between! … The Queen has a real <u>longing</u> to try it.[6]

The longing took root fast. Warming to the idea, the Queen now bombarded General Grey with quick-fire memos about it. In the first of two that she dashed off the following day, she said she had spoken to the outrider Trapp while on a drive and he had told her about a house called 'the Riss' in Tyrol in Austria which might be suitable: 'There is the <u>grandest</u> Alpine

---

* Her director of Continental Journeys.
† Governor to her son, Prince Arthur.

scenery in every direction and <u>complete</u> solitude. The Queen would prefer Switzerland as the Prince knew it and she would rather see nothing he had <u>not</u> seen, but on the other hand as <u>complete tranquility</u> and <u>solitude</u> is the chief object, that would be best obtained in the 'Riss'. Part of the suite would be left at the nearest Town.'[7]

Later that day she had an afterthought and wrote to Grey that she

> ... would wish General Grey not to be deterred by hearing of the smallness of accommodation, the distance from a town and the difficulty of provisions at the Riss. The Queen <u>can</u> and <u>would</u> put up with the homeliest food and provisions. She would take her meals (excepting perhaps breakfast and luncheon) with her very small suite; she would take only 1 gentleman and 1 lady & a Dr. besides her children – & <u>very few</u> servants. In <u>short</u> to live quite on a <u>reduced scale</u> and taking only those servants who would be <u>really useful</u>. The Queen has been calculating & if we can go in <u>one</u> night & a day from <u>here</u> ... the Queen thinks we might easily manage to come from Antwerp here without stopping; – we came purposely <u>slow</u> from Antwerp and Darmstadt & left very late. By leaving 3 or 4 hours earlier – & arriving here 2 hours later & going a little faster we might easily do it.[8]

So it was to be Austria.

Or perhaps Switzerland after all? But: 'It is the length of the journey,' she wrote to Grey the next day, 'wh. would make it necessary, if the Queen went to Switzerland, to spend 4 weeks there, or she could not undertake the journey.'[9]

Two days passed and it looked like Austria again, she told Grey, but staying at another house: '... a charming place ... . for the Queen to go to, wh. possesses <u>all</u> the advantages & none of the disadvantages of the Riss.'[10]

And so it went on. In the event, Queen Victoria did not go abroad at all in 1866, when Prussia and Austria were at war, nor in the following year. But by the summer of 1867 she was chafing at the bit again, determinedly laying plans for a few weeks in Switzerland in 1868, in deep seclusion. Prince Albert had toured there in 1837, before their marriage, and had sent her glowing accounts and mementos[11] that she treasured. In 1864 her third son, Prince Arthur, had followed in his father's footsteps around Switzerland.

A holiday in Switzerland, if well prepared, would bring her the much longed-for repose and seclusion she needed and at the same time she would be vicariously reunited with her beloved. But this powerful urge to get away from it all and steep herself in solitude, breathing the pure Alpine air that Albert had breathed, was in head-on conflict with an equally powerful pull in the opposite direction exerted by her subjects at home. They wanted more of her, not less.

Prince Arthur on his Swiss tour in 1864. The guide A. Hofmann is on right, with rope

Her courtiers had seen trouble brewing on this score for years. As far back as 1863 Viscount Torrington, one of her Lords-in-Waiting, had said as much in a letter to General Grey:

> ... there is strong pressure from without from almost the highest in the land down to the smallest boy in the streets of London to get the Queen once more to come to London. Loyalty, however inconvenient, is at the bottom of this movement. The public accept no one as a substitute and the danger is considerable if once that public cease to care or take an interest in seeing the Queen moving amongst them. It will not do for people to be accustomed to Her Majesty's absence. Do away with the outward and visible sign and the ignorant mass believe Royalty is of no value. There is not a tradesman in London who does not believe he is damaged by the Queen not coming to London.[12]

Yet here was Queen Victoria fighting tooth and nail to deprive her subjects of just these outward and visible signs of royalty – and feeling aggrieved that she was not given due credit for bearing up in spite of her widowed state and for conscientiously attending to the less public but onerous paperwork and discourse with ministers that her constitutional position thrust upon her. Even guardedly worded, constructively meant criticism of her reluctance to appear in public – even gentle persuasion that after some years of mourning she might now come more out of her shell again – all this aroused the Queen's grievous displeasure. She was especially allergic to such sentiments if they came from the press. 'She is shocked,' she wrote to General Grey in a memorandum, 'at the people treating her as an unfeeling machine, and how can they compare her to the Prince! He was a man, and had a happy home. She is a poor weak woman shattered by grief and anxiety and by nature terribly nervous! But she won't "heed" (as the Scotch say) those newspaper vulgarities and steadily do whatever _she_ can and she feels and thinks is fit. She would be thankful if the General would tell her when such articles _are_ in the papers, as then she won't read them.'[13]

But she did read them. The very next day she sent Grey another memorandum: 'Though the Queen promised General Grey not to read or take notice of those stupid unfeeling articles in the papers she can't resist sending him this one in the John Bull as she is rather amused at _Queen Emma of Honolulu_ being held up as an example to her! They seem rather to forget (and this is _always most astonishing_) that the _Queen_ has a _few_ other duties to perform than Queen Emma!! Please return the paper.'[14]

The Queen particularly dreaded having to open Parliament. Her letter on the subject to the then Prime Minister, Lord Russell, in early 1866 is something of a masterpiece in the way it combines commitment to her role as monarch with a passionate plea for mercy:

> To enable the Queen to go through what she can only compare to an execution, it is of importance to keep the thought of it as much from her mind as possible, and therefore the going to Windsor to wait two whole days for this dreadful ordeal would do her positive harm.
>
> The Queen has never till now mentioned this painful subject to Lord Russell, but she wishes once for all to just express her own feelings. She must, however, premise her observations by saying that she entirely absolves Lord Russell and his colleagues from any attempt ever to press upon her what is so very painful an effort. The Queen must say that she does feel very bitterly the want of feeling of those who ask the Queen to go to open Parliament. That the public should wish to see her she fully understands, and has no wish to prevent – quite the contrary; but why this wish should be of so unreasonable and unfeeling a nature as to long to witness the spectacle of a poor, broken-hearted widow, nervous and shrinking, dragged in deep mourning, alone in State as a Show, where she used to go supported by her husband, to be gazed at, without delicacy of feeling, is a thing she cannot understand, and she never could wish her bitterest foe to be exposed to!
>
> She will do it this time – as she promised it, but she owns she resents the unfeelingness of those who have clamoured for it. Of the suffering which it will cause her – nervous as she now is – she can give no idea, but she owns she hardly knows how she will go through it.[15]

She did manage – just.

> _Great crowds out, & so I had (for the first time since my great misfortune) an escort. Dressing after luncheon, which I could hardly touch. Wore my ordinary evening dress, only trimmed with miniver, and my cap with a long flowing tulle veil, a small diamond & sapphire coronet rather at the back, and diamonds outlining the front of my cap._
>
> _It was a fearful moment for me when I entered the carriage alone, and_

the band played; also when all the crowds cheered, and I had great difficulty in repressing my tears. But our two dear affectionate girls [Princesses Helena and Louise who faced the Queen in the carriage] were a true help & support to me, and they so thoroughly realised all I was going through. The crowds were most enthusiastic, & the people seemed to look at me with sympathy. We had both windows open, in spite of a very high wind.

When I entered the House which was very full, I felt as if I should faint. All was silent and all eyes fixed upon me, and there I sat alone. I was greatly relieved when all was over, & I stepped down from the throne ...

'*So thankful that the great ordeal of today was well over, & that I was enabled to get through it.*[16]

Queen Victoria opening Parliament, 1866

The press did not miss the opportunity to echo the growing public discontent with the Queen's seclusion – in fact, it fuelled the discontent. By 1867 feeling had exacerbated to such a degree that General Grey, in answer to the Queen's request that he should 'hint as to the harm' articles such as a recent one in *The Times* was doing,[17] felt impelled to tell her as gently as possible that, however much one understood her position, she was only making matters worse for herself:

... his distress on this occasion is much increased by feeling how little he can do to prevent its repetition. But where a feeling is very general, & very strong, it is difficult, if not impossible to prevent its finding expression; & General Grey would only be deceiving Your Majesty & concealing a truth of which Your Majesty ought to be aware, if he did not add that however unreasonable the feeling may be, & whatever may be thought of the time or manner in which it is expressed, or of the time chosen for expressing it, it is the fact that *The Times*, in this article has only followed the impulse given by, what General Grey cannot conceal from himself, is a very general & a very strong feeling.... People feel, very generally, that the tone of society is much deteriorated, & that unless some check is put upon its onward tendency, it will get worse & that very serious consequences may be the result. They believe that Your Majesty is the only person who has the power to interpose any effectual check upon this state of things, & that only by Your Majesty's resuming the place which none but Your Majesty can fill.[18]

This then is the background against which the Queen in great secrecy hatched her plot of escaping to Switzerland. During the summer and autumn of 1867 she conducted a lively correspondence with Howard Elphinstone, the Governor of Prince Arthur, about where to go the following summer. At first she still toyed with the idea of going to the Tyrol in Austria,[19] but she gave this up on learning how very remote the house in question was, what a long journey would be needed to reach it and how very hot it might be in that valley. An entry in her Journal in early August suggests that she still felt almost guilty about going away like this, in her widowed state, but could justify her urge for seclusion by invoking doctor's orders and expiate her feeling of guilt by going where Prince Albert had been in 1837:

> *Had a long talk with Maj. Elphinstone about a projected visit to Switzerland D.V. next year, which Dr. Jenner is most anxious I should undertake for my health, though it is terrible to do or see anything without my beloved Albert. Still I do long to see fine scenery, & Maj. Elphinstone is kindly going to try & find a nice place for me to go to.'*[20]

Elphinstone then suggested some possible places in Switzerland, to which the Queen replied in late August with a fairly clear specification.

The temperature of the places which Major Elphinstone mentions wld be

> totally unfit for the Queen, indeed – unless she can find bracing air – she wld <u>not</u> think of going to Switzerland <u>at all</u> – of course a <u>hot</u> sun and <u>hot</u> days she is prepared to put up with, but there must nevertheless <u>be</u> <u>fresh</u> & <u>cold</u> <u>air</u> besides.
>
> She wld put up with a <u>few small</u> houses supposing <u>only</u> she & her children, – maids & 2 or 3 menservants lived in <u>one</u>, the ladies & gentlemen in another, & so on; that wld do <u>perfectly</u> well – indeed she wld <u>like</u> <u>that</u> <u>best</u> – & any <u>little</u> alterations necessary she wld pay the expences for having made. <u>Only</u> let us find a <u>quiet</u> spot in true mountain scenery – with fine, <u>bracing</u>! air.[21]

The Queen ended this letter by saying she hoped the secret would be kept. A few days later she added to her specification.

> The Queen thanks Major Elphinstone for <u>all</u> his letters & <u>all</u> the gt. & kind trouble he has taken to further her wishes. ... She will be most curious to hear all from him as to the possibilities afforded for her going to Switzerland. But later than the beginning of Aug. She c.ld not go there – nor w.ld she wish to remain longer than the 10th or 12th of Sept. It w.ld else prevent her getting <u>enough</u> of the bracing Highland air. 6 weeks of the <u>latter</u> she w.ld <u>wish</u> to have.[22]

Elphinstone went to Switzerland on a reconnaissance journey and duly reported back in October with a memorandum containing descriptions of two houses on the Lake of Lucerne that might be suitable. 'He regrets however that he cannot give further details. – It was impossible ... to procure these, because, both the houses being private residences admittance could not be obtained without disclosing the object of the visit.'[23]

The private house idea was dropped, but not the location. Although Elphinstone, a careful courtier, does not presume further than that 'Your Majesty has to some extent made up Your mind whereabouts You would wish to remain',[24] the Queen's sights were in fact now firmly set on central Switzerland and she pursued this aim with ruthless determination until August 1868, in the face of all the obstacles the first half of that year was to put in her way.

These obstacles were formidable. There were dramatic political developments that demanded the presence of the monarch at the seat of government and the press was turning nasty. The Conservative government was in a minority in the House of Commons, the ailing Prime Minister Lord Derby resigned in February (to die the following year) and the prospect of a General Election loomed throughout the year. This deprived the Queen of any certainty that she would long enjoy the one stroke of good fortune that fate had vouchsafed her for years: a congenial Prime Minister in the person of Benjamin Disraeli who stepped up from being Chancellor of the Exchequer to replace Lord Derby. Disraeli knew the value of General Grey as a frank and fearless counsellor and wrote imploring him to stay on when Grey had begun to despair of ever persuading the Queen that she needed to make more public appearances.

> ... After we lost the Prince, which seemed to me, at first an irrecoverable blow in the conduct of public affairs, I have always looked to you as the principal means by which public business might be carried on with satisfaction to Ministers individually, and advantage to the State. It seems to me almost an act of Providence, that the Queen's private confidence should have devolved upon a real gentleman; a man of honor, intelligence, and acquirements; and of no mean experience of life, and especially of political life. I should myself deplore, as a great misfortune, your secession from Her Majesty's service.[25]

Grey's answer dwelt on the need to feel that he was being treated with confidence:

> The mere suspicion that such is not the case, necessarily impairs, if it does not destroy one's usefulness, and renders such a situation as mine altogether intolerable. I cannot conceal from myself that since, on more occasions than one, I have given unpalatable opinions to the Queen, she is become reserved with me, and, in certain questions now shuts herself up with me entirely. I believe, however, that this proceeds less from any diminution of confidence, than the fears of having things pressed upon her which jar with her inclinations; and it is this belief chiefly, which induces me still to hold on in a position which, as I told you when you were here, is become very disagreeable to me.'

The letter continues with gloomy foreboding:

> I wish I could think matters would mend but if, as I am determined to do, I do my duty to the Queen, honestly, I foresee that they will only become worse. However, you may be sure that I shall do nothing hastily, and I am much cheered and encouraged in holding on, by the kind and flattering manner in which you have expressed yourself towards me.

The end of this letter, however, holds out a glimmer of hope: 'Since I wrote this letter I have received from the Queen (for the first time for some weeks!) instructions which certainly go to show no want of confidence, however certain subjects may be tabooed, and though she may prefer not to hold personal communication with me!'[26]

Grey stayed on, but neither he nor Disraeli nor anyone or anything else (including the sniping of the press) could dissuade her from making things worse by resolving to go in May for some weeks to Balmoral, her residence in Scotland. Disraeli tried – yet, as he said to Grey, 'she ought not to go to Scotland, but she will'.[27] And she did. Grey had all the more reason to be anxious for the Queen because he was one of the very few people who knew that not very long after returning from Balmoral she would be heading for the Continent.

In fairness to the Queen, she had real cause for grief and anxiety on top of her self-imposed burden of honouring the memory of her dear departed with her own brand of perpetual mourning. It was taking her years to recover her balance after being deprived of her Consort, her pillar of strength. In March 1868 her second son Prince Alfred was shot and wounded in Australia by a member of the Irish Republican movement called the Fenian Brotherhood. In April she was praying for the success of a British expeditionary force against Theodore, King of Abyssinia, who had taken hostage all the British subjects he could lay his hands on in the country. Her prayers were heard: the force advanced through an almost impassable region to Theodore's fortress of Magdala and released the prisoners.

Benjamin Disraeli

At the beginning of May a violent political upheaval was triggered by Gladstone's Liberal Opposition carrying a Resolution in the House of Commons that the Irish branch of the United Church of England and Ireland should be disestablished, since it ministered to only a very small minority. The Liberals knew that the Government could not act on a constitutional issue such as this without going to the country. Sure enough, Disraeli advised the Queen to dissolve Parliament and told her that, if she should think it best, Ministers were ready to resign at once. The Queen (understandably) refused the offer of resignation, but agreed that there should in due course be a dissolution and General Election. This finally happened in November and she spent the summer and autumn anxiously hoping that her new ally and supporter Disraeli would not be swept from office, to be replaced by the much less sympathetic Gladstone.

It is ironic that in May Disraeli of all people should have – no doubt unthinkingly – given her a cruel reminder of this possibility, in the course of a letter full of flowery thanks. The Queen had (decorously via an intermediary to Mrs Disraeli) sent him spring flowers 'as they will make his room look so bright'. Writing from the House of Commons, Disraeli immediately thanked the Queen 'for your Majesty's bright and gracious recollection of him this morn. None of the decorations, on which he sometimes has to take your Majesty's pleasure, were half as fair; and he trusts, that in their sweetness and their beauty, they may ever be typical of your Majesty's life and thoughts.' But Disraeli rather marred the effect by saying in the same letter ' ... The House very serene, and about to die'.[28] Reminding the Queen of a distasteful prospect was no doubt the last thing he had in mind; but he will have been anxious to shield her from the unpleasant truth, which was that serenity was in fact in very short supply in Parliament. The place was in turmoil – as vividly portrayed by *The Globe and Traveller* on 19 May:

> *Will there be a Dissolution?*
> The temper of the Opposition becomes more splenetic and venomous every day. Whatever the PRIME MINISTER proposes, MR GLADSTONE and his allies are resolved, if possible, to thwart. Never before have the annals of the House of Commons been disgraced by party warfare so thoroughly sordid and unscrupulous. Never before has a politician – for MR GLADSTONE has forfeited every claim to be called a statesman – exhibited in a form so despicable the mingled results of personal dislike and disappointed ambition. The spirit of envy has taken mortal shape, and represents South Lancashire.

South Lancashire was Gladstone's parliamentary seat. *The Globe* supported the Conservative Party.

To add to the Queen's worries, the press had now become even more outspoken than before in its strictures on her absences from the centre of affairs. She was particularly aggrieved when one such article appeared in *The Globe* in mid-May, just after she had made a great effort by not only entertaining at Buckingham Palace but also laying the foundation stone of the new St Thomas's Hospital in London. The article acknowledged these public activities as the dawn of a new spring in relations between the Sovereign and her loyal subjects, but deplored her intention of nipping it in the bud by betaking herself away again almost at once.

> *The Queen with her Subjects*
> It is with no feigned satisfaction or perfunctory sense of duty that we chronicle the graceful discharge of one of the most important functions of Royalty by HER MAJESTY yesterday. The deep shade of sorrow which the death of the illustrious and much-loved PRINCE CONSORT cast on the SOVEREIGN and Court of England has for some time obscured the lustre of the Crown. ... The people ... ever and anon ... have looked hopefully and anxiously to see the Monarch ... rise from the sombre shade and once more appear before her people with bright, if chastened mien; resuming the responsibilities of her exalted station, and again performing the duties of her peerless state....
>
> The monarch is not only the ruler but also the head of the nation. In the wearer of the Crown centre the force and vitality of the national body corporate. From the occupant of the Throne, as from a fountain, flows all honour. From the dynast depends all dignity. What the sun is in the planetary system the SOVEREIGN is to the social system.... If the head is clouded in grief, the whole body suffers. If the fountain flows feebly, honour is at a low ebb. If the dynast is hidden from view, dignity comes to be disregarded. If the sun is eclipsed, vigour, growth, and harmony are endangered in the social system.
>
> ... With profound respect ... we venture to give expression to the desire that an impression to the effect that HER MAJESTY meditates an early departure for her far-off home in the Highlands may even now prove unfounded. ... A Royal birthday spent in the Highlands ... withdrawn from us would doubtless be enjoyable to the Royal Family, but in some sort a misfortune to the nation.

The Queen reacted violently. On the day this article appeared she wrote a defensive letter to Disraeli, saying she was prepared to return earlier than contemplated from Scotland 'if anything ... very serious should render it necessary – but she is completely done up by the fatigue of these few days ... [She has had so] much anxiety & worry during the last 2 or 3 years of every kind & sort that it is beginning to tell very seriously on her health & nerves – wh. are both very much shaken – ... The Queen would not have written all this to Mr. Disraeli now, had she not been much annoyed & pained at an article in this Govt's *Globe*, (wh. she understands is a Govt. paper) wh. she considers a most ungrateful return for the very gt. exertions she has made this season ...[29]

On this day the Queen also appealed to Theodore Martin, a man of influence with the press:

Mr Martin has been so kind and feeling, and knowing so well how the Queen's health and nerves are shaken – therefore will understand how very great the efforts made this year have been – a week in London, three Drawing-rooms, and the great ceremony yesterday, from which she is suffering much to-day; he will accordingly not be surprised at the indignation and pain with which she read the Article in *The Globe* to-night, and her great anxiety therefore that he or Mr Helps should try and prevent similar Articles appearing in *The Times* and *Daily Telegraph*. Every increased effort is rewarded by such shameless Articles; and the discouragement and pain they cause are very great. ... Were she not to get away for three to four weeks (and no public service can suffer, for communication is very rapid) she believes she would completely break down. They even grudge the Prince of Wales going down for three days to spend his poor widowed mother's birthday with her (for the first time since '61!). It is very cruel! The Queen hears it is not at all the general feeling, and that people are really anxious about her; but she really is feeling utterly worn out; and does wish some newspaper would point out how much she has done, and how necessary it is to keep her well enough to go on, for else she may be unable to do so.[30]

Her appeal failed. Six days later *The Times* thundered forth. In stinging phrases the article lambasted the Prime Minister for not impressing on the Queen the necessity for her, as constitutional Head of State, to be at hand at this time of political crisis:

On Monday night the Queen's Ministers were twice defeated in the House of Commons. ... There is a Ministerial crisis, which may dissolve either the Ministry or the Parliament. This being the state of things, the public has been astonished by another contemporary incident. In the same paper of yesterday which contained the news of MR DISRAELI's defeat and his motion to report progress on the Scotch Reform Bill it was announced that the QUEEN, with her family, had left Windsor Castle the evening before, at half-past 6 o'clock, for Balmoral. Thus, at the very hour when a most important debate was proceeding – a debate on which the question of life and death to Government or to Parliament might turn – the first person in the State, to whom recourse must be had in every momentous juncture, was hurrying at full speed from the neighbourhood of the capital to a remote Highland district, six hundred miles from her Ministry and Parliament. In the month of May, at a time when the business of the Nation is at its height, and interests of every kind cause people to congregate in London – at a time when it is especially necessary that the SOVEREIGN should be accessible to her Ministers and to the Legislature, we have the whole Court withdrawn to a distance which renders any personal communication impossible.... MR DISRAELI is 63 years of age, and, though mentally energetic, it would be too much to ask him to rush to the Highlands at

Balmoral Castle from the opposite side of the Dee

Limited Mail speed and return within 48 hours. So HER MAJESTY must be communicated with by messenger, if at all; and, however the communication is made there must be an inconvenient lapse of time before the answer is received....

We must think, therefore, that it was an act of culpable neglect on the part of the Minister not to inform the QUEEN that the political prospects of her government were so doubtful as to demand her presence at or near the seat of the Legislature....

There was worse to come. The next day a report was telegraphed to Balmoral of an extraordinary incident in Parliament. An MP had in the House of Commons formally raised the question of her abdication, by asking 'whether it be true that HM the Queen has been compelled through delicate health to retire from England during the remainder of this session; and if so, whether it is the intention of Her Majesty's Government, out of consideration to Her Majesty's health, comfort and tranquility, and in the interest of the Royal Family and of HM's subjects throughout the Empire, and especially of this Metropolis, to advise Her Majesty to abdicate.'[31]

This Question, in the words of the *Pall Mall Gazette*, 'was received with a condemnatory shout of "order" from all quarters of the House, was rebuked by the Speaker for the disrespectful terms of the question and [the MP] apologized for his offence against the good taste and the etiquette of Parliament'.

The Queen felt goaded beyond endurance. She followed up her letter to

Disraeli with another – a letter that contained the ultimate threat:

> She <u>thinks</u> it vy important that the question of her <u>state</u> of health <u>once</u> for <u>all</u> shld. be <u>understood</u>. – It is simply this: The Queen's health – & nerves – <u>require</u> in the spring time a <u>short interval</u> of bracing mountain air & comparative quiet – or she <u>must</u> break down completely & <u>if</u> the public will <u>not</u> take her – as she is – she must <u>give all up</u> – & give it up to the Pr. of Wales. – No doubt they wld. wish her to be always in London for <u>their</u> convenience … but the Queen <u>can't</u>…. The Queen's looks belie her & <u>nobody</u> believes <u>how</u> she suffers.[32]

Facsimile of pages from Queen Victoria's letter of 22 May 1868 to Disraeli, in which she threatens to abdicate

The Queen asked Disraeli to have the matter authoritatively raised in consultation with her physician, Sir William Jenner, adding in a dig at General Grey that it ought to have been done long ago and that her own people had 'never been wise or judicious in this'.[33]

Queen Victoria was certainly right in thinking that her looks belied her real condition. General Grey, writing to his wife about the gilly* dance on the occasion of the Queen's birthday in the last week of May, rather unchivalrously bore out her point: 'Princess Louise looked really lovely at the dance, and tho' H.M. did <u>not</u>, no one who saw her could <u>for a moment</u> have surmised that her <u>health</u> required care!'[34]

* Grey's spelling.

But of course the Queen's state of mind was a different matter.

As the turbulent month of May drew to a close the tide of public censure had turned and was beginning to ebb. The Sovereign's Birthday on 24 May saw the press handsomely – but still guardedly – making amends for their earlier strictures, in an outburst of loyalty and understanding for her parlous condition; the Queen was also much comforted by a letter from her eldest daughter, the Crown Princess of Prussia. 'Your dear, loving, warm-hearted letter of the 20th,' she wrote back, 'reached me on the morning of my poor, sad ... birthday – so full of recollections – so far off. The <u>present</u> has now become a reality & is like a different life. You speak so dearly & affectionately & I do so long to fold you to my heart – <u>my</u> <u>own</u> <u>own</u> <u>own</u> loved <u>1st born</u>! – but you <u>must</u> <u>bear</u> with your poor old Mama, for her head gets so tired & she is so fagged & wasted that I fear you will find her a dull, tiresome companion....

'But I do gratefully accept what God <u>has</u> sent to cheer ... & comfort me.'[35]

During the rest of her month at Balmoral the Queen did not fail to study and react to the long accounts of the Parliamentary Debates prepared for her by Grey and the hurried appraisals sent by Disraeli. As usual she also conscientiously dealt with all the voluminous paperwork that came her way. While all this was going on she must have been wondering how she was going to break the news of yet another absence – and half way across Europe at that – relatively soon after returning to England. Throughout these troubled months she had clung tenaciously, as if to a lifeline, to her project of escaping to Switzerland for a complete rest and change. But she had shared the secret with only two or three people, those concerned with the arrangements that were being made for the journey and accommodation.

Even these few were too many. Writing to her mother from Potsdam in early June, the Crown Princess, Victoria, said she had heard from her father-in-law, the King of Prussia, that 'you are coming to Switzerland in August. Is that true?'[36] The Queen wrote a damage-limitation letter explaining her need for secrecy,[37] but she must have spent the month having nightmares about the cat being let out of the bag in London and turning into a fierce British lion that roared its disapproval of her abandoning her realm for foreign climes.

Victoria, Crown Princess of Prussia, the Queen's eldest daughter

Scotland did her good: she felt stronger and better for it and had to tear herself away, as she wrote to the Crown Princess on her last night, adding: 'It is now near 11 – & still vy light – there is such charm in that soft, clear light.'[38]

Back in Windsor, the Queen found life even more unbearable than she had feared. Not only did she have to take part publicly in the dreaded English Season, but she had come straight from the invigorating air of her beloved Scottish glens and forests into a fierce heatwave. Her body was built for cool weather, not high temperatures, and she suffered accordingly. Hardly an entry in her Journal or a letter of hers at this time is without some reference to the heat and what it was doing to her.

But she soldiered on. June 20 found her taking a one-and-a-half hour march-past of 24,000 troops. *Very tired but greatly pleased and gratified* says her Journal. Yet on the same day she wrote to the Crown Princess that 'the heat is so fearful today that I can hardly hold my pen ... so unwell with violent headaches and sickness since I came back that I am quite shaky.'[39]

Two days later she faced the music again and went to Buckingham Palace for a monster Garden Party.

At 5 the alarming moment arrived & I went down into the garden.... Quantities of people on the lawn whom I had to recognize as I went along & after nearly 8 years seclusion, it was vy. puzzling & bewildering.[40]

There were Tyrolean singers and a band. The Queen talked and had tea with the Royal party in a tent. *This over, I slowly walked back to the Palace, talking to people on the way. Felt quite exhausted & faint & I had seemed to be in a dream, so totally unsuited to the scene.*[41]

Twenty-four hours were enough for her at Buckingham Palace. She was back at Windsor by the following afternoon and sweltered there ('overpowered by the heat') until she could decently get away to her island retreat of Osborne, on the Isle of Wight, where it was no less oppressive but at least she was away from Windsor, 'that dungeon'.[42]

There should have been one more ordeal before she could be released to go to Switzerland: the Speech from the Throne proroguing the Parliamentary Session until the autumn. But fate was kind to her and the speech was delivered on her behalf by the Lords Commissioners. The speech, drafted as usual by the Government, had of course been submitted to her. In her Journal of 30 July she wrote of holding a Privy Council *before which I saw Mr. Disraeli, who spoke kindly about the speech, saying that he felt so grateful to me for suggesting a slight alteration in the last paragraph, which I thought as it 1st stood might have fettered the Govt. in any future liberal policy. All the Cabinet agreed about the alteration, but none had thought about it.*

So that was satisfactorily dealt with. Furthermore, the Season was drawing to a close, and those who could were intent upon getting away for country pursuits. As *The Gentleman's Magazine* put it: 'The London Season begins with the reprieve of the partridges and the pheasants, and ends with the death warrant of the grouse.'

One major problem remained. The solution proposed for it was about to be put to the test.

2 *Incognita*

The big question-mark still hanging over Queen Victoria's Swiss holiday as she prepared for departure in early August 1868 concerned her urgent need for privacy. Was she going to travel half way across Europe, braving a record heat-wave in order to recruit her health and strength in glorious surroundings, only to be plagued by the very public attention she was trying to escape from? Was she going to find the total seclusion she so desperately sought? Time would soon tell, but meanwhile she at least had the satisfaction of knowing that she had all along taken every possible precaution.

Total secrecy was out of the question. If she had ever thought that she could make such a journey secretly and go undetected for a month in a country crawling with her own subjects as well as holidaymakers from far and wide, she would soon have abandoned the thought. Of course the Swiss hotel-keepers and staff already then knew what was good for them: travellers high and low could rely implicitly on their absolute discretion. But the public at large, although by that time used to the spectacle of foreign grandees lording it in their resorts, might have taken more than a passing interest in a personality as well known as the Queen of England. And she could hardly have gone about in disguise.

So the Queen did the obvious thing. She changed her name. In doing so she took advantage of a convention as practical then as it is paradoxical to us today, a device breathing the spirit of an age that observed a well-defined – and in many ways genial – code of conduct: the incognito. By announcing that she was going abroad as 'The Countess of Kent', the Queen was letting it be known that she was not expecting to be treated as Queen, but as an (almost) ordinary traveller.

To our modern ears the very word incognito has the distant echo of a long-vanished age of manners. For Queen Victoria the device was a readily available possibility, and it promised relief from torment. It was marvellously effective: all she had to do was to announce she was going incognita and governments would take no official notice of her, the press would stay at a safe distance and the public would not pry. Everyone would know who she was, but nobody would bother her, since she would be going about as an unknown countess. The authorities were thereby elegantly absolved from the need of paying their respects to a Head of State, and the press and public were implicitly requested to leave her in peace.

Queen Victoria had used the device before, and it had worked reasonably well. She was now fervently hoping that it would serve her even better at this agonizing time for her escape to Switzerland – an escape which had taken three long years to become a reality. Although at the outset in 1865 she had considered both Switzerland and Austria, Switzerland was the obvious choice. Apart from its growing fame as 'the Garden of England', it was where Prince Albert had toured in 1837 – a sojourn from which he had sent the young Queen he was soon to marry several mementos.[43] She kept these, which included a pressed Alpine rose from the Rigi, in an album which she said she took with her wherever she went. Then, in 1864, her son Prince Arthur with his Governor Major Elphinstone had gone on what amounted to a sentimental journey, following the same route and very much encouraged by his mother.

High in the Queen's esteem for his discretion and loyalty, Howard Elphinstone put his knowledge of other countries and their languages to work in order to find suitable accommodation for her in Switzerland

Clearly the Queen had to go to Switzerland. In 1867 when she started planning in earnest, Elphinstone was the obvious person to recruit as a fellow-plotter. She was uneasily aware that it was going to be difficult to sell the idea to her subjects, who were already discontented at her withdrawal from public life and all-too-frequent absences from her capital. But she also felt, at heart, that she was not yet ready to be fully back in the swim. Thus, come what may, she was determined to do what she needed – to get away whenever she could. However, she was anxious to postpone for as long as possible the difficult moment of issuing an announcement.

The first thing was to decide where to go. Elphinstone threw himself into the task with enthusiasm, suggesting a host of possible destinations. The Queen rejected them all for being too hot. So he set off to reconnoitre in Switzerland and recommended two private houses he had 'cased' near the Lake of Lucerne. These too were rejected and the search was resumed early in the following year, 1868.

The Queen knew what she wanted when she wrote to Elphinstone:

> The simplest fare, 2 of my cooks enough. Probably the Queen would take 2 Ponies and a carriage, but no horses. Inquire as to what the carriages of the country are. Perhaps some new cushions might make them comfortable enough not to necessitate the Queen taking her own carriage which would probably not be so useful for that country – Are the horses always driven from the box or not? It would be more convenient if there were room for 2 on the box – as the Queen would not feel safe if she had not Brown with her, and he would not be able to communicate with the people nor would he know the country. Inquiries must be made as to the water etc....[44]

Towards the end of March the Queen, still moving only within the tiny circle of those in the know, sent a memorandum to General Grey in which she, almost hesitantly for her, broached a subject that she knew very well was going to spell trouble: two long summer absences.

> With regard to what she stated yesterday she would just repeat in writing what she said. Sir William Jenner wishes the Queen to have 4 weeks or a months complete change of scene and as much mental rest as possible, and for that (not to break in upon some weeks of the bracing Highland air which is equally necessary to her health) it is essential she should not be detained in England beyond the 7th or 8th August: and she is therefore anxious to know whether something could not be done (as it is a case of health) to permit this, should Parliament be prolonged beyond that period.
> The Queen's whole system her nerves, stomach etc are all very much shaken by the 6 years and more of unassisted labour and responsibility, added to the terrible grief which for the first 3 or 4 years quite overpowered her strength; then came years of much anxiety both public, and domestic and last year especially she was very sorely tried in many ways.
> She feels it a duty to her family and people to do all to prevent her getting worse and becoming incapable of continuing her duties at all'.[45]

What the Queen was after in this letter was to anticipate and get round a potential show-stopper: could she go abroad with Parliament still in session? And there were other considerations. Queen Victoria, although not Head of Government, at that time still exercised more direct influence on decisions than in her later years. Apart from that, the Royal Assent was (and is) needed for every piece of legislature. When the Lord Chancellor, Lord Cairns, was consulted on the subject, he produced a splendid Opinion:

Absence of the Sovereign from Her Dominions
Confidential Memorandum
It was formerly the custom, when the Sovereign was about to leave the Kingdom, to appoint Lords Justices, by Letters Patent under the Great Seal, to exercise during the absence of the Sovereign certain portions of the Royal Prerogative.

The last occasion when this was done was in 1821, when His late Majesty King George the 4th was about to proceed on a visit to the Continent.

Since that time, no appointment of Lords Justices has been made.

When Her Majesty was about to visit Germany in 1845, the late Lord Campbell, in the House of Lords, enquired whether Lords Justices would be appointed, and suggested that it would be unconstitutional not to do so. The Lord Chancellor (Lord Lyndhurst) said the question had been carefully considered both on that occasion, and also when Her Majesty had visited France; and that the Government, acting on the advice of the Law Officers, were of opinion that there was no Law or rule requiring the appointment of Lords Justices; that a Secretary of State would attend Her Majesty; and that the increased facilities of communications made the former precedents no longer applicable.

The latter reason is, at the present time, still more forcible.

Beyond, therefore, the regular communications between Her Majesty and Her Majesty's Ministers for the purpose of taking Her Majesty's Pleasure, and obtaining the Royal Sign Manual – which can be conducted with more or less dispatch according to the exigency of the case – the only matter which requires to be considered is the Royal Assent to Bills in Parliament.

There can be no General Commission to give Assent to Bills: nor can there be a Commission to assent to a Bill until the Bill has passed all its stages in both Houses – There will probably be ample time to transmit and return Commissions in regular course for all Bills other than the Appropriation Bill.

As to the Appropriation Bill, it is generally the last which passes through the Houses of Parliament; and, when it has passed, both Houses must wait until the Commission with the Royal Sign Manual is returned.

Any delay as to this, would be best avoided by sending beforehand to the Secretary of State, or Minister in attendance on Her Majesty, a Commission, with the date in blank, for giving Assent to the Appropriation Bill. On the Bill passing the last stage, a telegraphic message could be sent to the Secretary of State, who would insert the date in the Commission; submit it for Her Majesty's Signature; and at once transmit it by Special Messenger to the Lord

Chancellor. Probably all this could be done in 24 or 36 hours.[46]

Most satisfactory, if wordy. It meant that the Queen was let off the hook even if Parliament were still in session when she went to Switzerland – an increasingly likely eventuality in view of the uncertain political situation.

Her immediate problem was to get through the spring with all its anxieties and do whatever possible to win understanding for her month in Balmoral from May to June.

By early June she had weathered the Balmoral storm and was feeling calmer. So it must have been a real blow to her when a letter arrived at the beginning of June from her eldest daughter Crown Princess Victoria in Germany asking whether it was true that she was going to Switzerland in August.[47] Realizing that her cover had been blown, the Queen wrote back:

> I am very much surprised at what the King told you about my plans. Of course for very long I was very uncertain as to what I cld. do – but Sir Wm Jenner was very anxious I shld. go to Switzerland quite incognita, & as quietly as possible – for a complete change of Scene – thinking it might do my nerves good. But I told no one, except those 2 or 3 on whose secrecy I can implicitly rely. I can receive no one, neither children, relations or acquaintances, for else it becomes what the Rosenau was each time – a gt. fatigue and excitement. You will at once, dear Child, see the necessity for this line being drawn. I wld. have told you before – but having to keep it quiet as long as possible here …[48]

The Crown Princess then replied that 'I quite understand your journey to Switzerland, indeed I did so before you told me about it, it was Ct. Bernstorff*[49] who wrote it in an official despatch a week or 2 ago. I hope it may do you good and what an enjoyment is in store for you.'

No doubt; but first there were troubled waters to sail through. It was now clear that the moment of truth was upon her: an announcement would have to be made fairly soon – especially since she had finally decided upon her accommodation in Lucerne and arrangements for the journey itself had to be got under way. Perhaps the trip could be kept under wraps a little longer, at least until she had made her eagerly awaited public appearances in London. But she could at least share her thoughts about it with the Crown Princess. ' … You shall hear all about my Journey – but I am going to see no sights. All Picture Galleries & Exhibitions as a rule I have been obliged to give up – as I am quite unequal to them. I am able for very little & I don't think I shall be

---

* Sure enough, Count Bernstorff, the long-time Prussian Ambassador to London, had somehow winkled out the secret and reported on 30 May (in French, as protocol demanded) that arrangements had been made for the Queen to spend August in Switzerland. Of Lord Stanley, though, he only said that he would spend the Parliamentary recess 'in the country'.[49]

able to make any long excursions – for I get tired very easily & <u>sun</u> heat I positively <u>cannot</u> bear. Your 2 sisters & Leopold – my <u>inseparables</u> go with me. It is to <u>Lucerne</u> that I am going (please don't betray this) & I have taken the Pension Wallis <u>there</u> …'[50]

Staying in a pension on the Continent was a radical departure for the Queen. On her previous trips abroad she had always stayed in residences belonging to members of her family. The Pension Wallis belonged to Robert Wallis, an English lithographer who had moved to Lucerne from his birthplace in Germany and had married a local Swiss woman. Although originally something of a hot-head and radical when first in Switzerland during the momentous 1840s, he had settled down and established a successful lithography business. This enabled him to branch out and build a select, intimate 'pension', which opened for business in 1866. The whole of it was rented for the Queen's stay. Commanding glorious views over the lake, the house occupied a prime site on a hill called the Gütsch, just outside the town.

With an admirably secluded Swiss base thus secured, the next step was to

Lucerne, seen from the Gütsch

ensure privacy while travelling. Wheels were set in motion to this end on 1 July, when General Grey wrote a private letter to Disraeli:

> As the time is now approaching, within 5 or 6 weeks, when the Queen intends to go abroad in search of that peace & repose which the state of her health renders so essential, I write to you, by Her Majesty's desire, to say that Her Majesty has fixed upon a residence about 1/2 an hour, or 3/4 of an hour distant from Lucerne, & will proceed there in the first days of August.
>
> In order to derive the full benefit from this excursion, it is absolutely necessary that Her Majesty's privacy should not be unnecessarily disturbed. She therefore proposes to travel under a real, not a half & half, incognita, as when she went to Coburg, & I will let you know, as soon as it has been decided on, the name under which it will be her pleasure to travel.
>
> It is Her Majesty's wish to be treated entirely as a Private Individual, going abroad for her health, & it is therefore her intention resolutely to decline every offer of anything like Royal Honours, & all visits that may be offered by Relations, or Members of Foreign Royal families. I write in the same sense to Ld. Stanley,* to beg that he will clearly explain his wishes in this respect to Mr Lumley,† & to request that he will not only use his own best endeavours, but try to obtain the cooperation of the local authorities, whenever it may be necessary, to prevent her being intruded upon by the world.
>
> It is from her desire to secure this quiet that H. M. has hitherto been silent on the subject of her intention to go to Switzerland, & she trusts with entire confidence in you to do whatever may be in your powers to further Her wishes.
>
> Nothing will probably be going on during H.M.'s absence. Parlt. will be up, & you will be all preparing for the coming Elections, while all seems peaceable on the Continent. She does not know, therefore, that the presence of a Minister will be necessary. But should you think it unadvisable that H.M. shd. remain for four weeks abroad, without being in reach of one of her responsible Advisers, one of the Ministers might easily come out to Lucerne, as for his private convenience; & there he is, as I have already said, at only 1/2 an hour, or 3/4 of an hour's distance from Her Majesty. – I will write again, about the mode of communicating with the Queen while abroad. I will only say now that, in order to preserve her incognita inviolate, H.M. does not wish anything to be addressed to her as <u>Queen.</u>
>
> Yrs very truly
> C. Grey

* The Foreign Secretary.
† The British Minister to Switzerland in Berne.

Since writing the above the Queen has expressed a wish that the Ld. Chancellor shd. be asked whether there would be any objection to Her Majesty assuming the title, when abroad, of Countess of Chester. The P. of Wales is Earl of Chester. – H.M. does not wish to take the title of Dss. of Lancaster under which she has before travelled, & which is not favourable to the strict incognita she desires to maintain.[51]

There was an objection: the Princess of Wales was Countess of Chester and the Queen could hardly hijack one of her daughter-in-law's titles (although, as Sovereign, she theoretically was entitled to do so). The upshot of the ensuing consultation was that the Lord Chancellor, Lord Cairns, wrote to Disraeli that 'The Duke of Edinburgh is Earl of Kent: so that if Her Majesty thought fit to use the Style of Countess of Kent, the difficulty as to the title of Countess of Chester, arising from that being one of the dignities of the Princess of Wales, would be avoided.'[52]

On 7 July the Queen's Journal records a discussion with Disraeli: ... *Talked of my journey abroad & my taking the title of Css. of Kent, a fine old title & now one of Affie's.*[53] Affie, her second son, was Prince Alfred, Duke of Edinburgh and of Saxe-Coburg-Gotha.

Later that month it was finally judged opportune to issue a public announcement about her forthcoming journey, the wording having been decided upon after correspondence between General Grey (its drafter), Disraeli and a hesitant Queen.

The Queen will leave England early next month for a short residence in Switzerland.

As Her Majesty goes abroad entirely on the recommendation of her Physicians, in search of the change of air and repose which they consider so essential to her health – she will maintain the strictest incognita during her absence – refusing even the visits, as well as the attentions usually paid to Sovereigns when travelling on the Continent and in such circumstances.[54]

This news was, of course, immediately seized upon by the press, but by this time the sting had (for the time being) been drawn from the long-standing feud about her absences. For one thing, the ground had been well prepared this time (after the Queen's sternly expressed annoyance that the public relations aspect of her earlier stay in Scotland had been bungled by Court and Government). For another, the London Season was coming to an end. The gentry were heading for their country places – and, indeed, many of them for Switzerland (as were increasing numbers of less privileged people). So there were no reproaches.

The Globe, 1 August 1868
THIS MONTH'S INTELLIGENCE
The Queen will leave Osborne on Wednesday for a short residence in Switzerland, under the advice of Sir William Jenner, who will accompany Her Majesty. Lord Stanley will leave London a few days afterwards, and will be at Her Majesty's commands. Her Majesty will maintain a strict incognita during her residence so that Her Majesty may be able to command a few weeks of complete repose which, with change of air, is deemed highly necessary for Her Majesty's health.

The day before this article appeared Disraeli had written to the Foreign Secretary, Lord Stanley: 'Remember to exercise your large influence with the Press, to say as little about our friend as possible.'[55]

Stanley did so to good effect. He was the Cabinet Minister appointed to be at hand in Switzerland in order to transact any public business requiring the Queen, but also to keep unwanted visitors (that is, everybody) from her doorstep. Stanley was an odd choice. The heir to the Earldom of Derby, he was a living example of the gulf between the old British landed aristocracy and a Royal Family not yet pukka in their eyes. He inclined to defeatism and was something of a pessimist. On hearing of the Queen's intention to get away from it all in Switzerland, his first reaction (noted in his diary) was characteristic: 'A strange report that the Queen is going to pass a month in Switzerland. If true, she will give offence to the Irish, who expect a visit: and to the Emperor, as she will not pass thro' Paris: while she will be mobbed by tourists of all nations, and half killed with heat, which always, as she says, makes her ill.'[56] Hardly balm to the ear of a Queen already jittery over this aspect of her forthcoming tour.

Lord Stanley, Foreign Secretary

When Stanley went to Windsor to present the Brazilian Minister, he observed: 'The Queen well, but growing enormously fat: complains much of her health: talks of her Swiss tour &c. I warn her against heat and tourists, by whom she will be mobbed to any amount.'[57]

Stanley was, to say the least, an indifferent performer in Parliament. *The Times* wrote of one of his speeches during this disastrous 1868 session '... His amendment was smothered in his own confusion.' *The Gentleman's Magazine*, although admitting that with him 'you may always reckon upon sound manly sense', called his articulation 'terribly disconcerting. It is zigzag and blurred.'

Draft of Lord Stanley's letter to the British Minister in Berne, as amended by the Queen

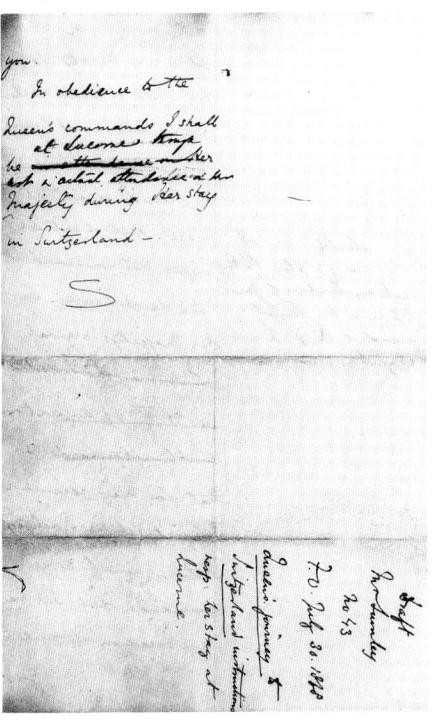

Yet he was, after all, Foreign Secretary and the logical choice to be Minister in Attendance. However, the Queen could do without his kind of encouragement. She was prepared to tolerate him – but at arm's length. When she saw the letter he had drafted to the British Legation in Berne, the Swiss Federal capital, announcing that he would be 'in attendance on the Queen',[58] she firmly crossed out this phrase and inserted her own amendment – as a result of which the letter that actually went to Berne had her revised wording: 'In obedience to the Queen's commands I shall be at Lucerne though not in actual attendance on Her Majesty during Her stay in Switzerland.'[59]

The earlier part of this letter to Berne spells out the ground rules laid down for the way the Queen's visit was to be treated by officials in Switzerland.

> I have already informed you that the Queen proposes to pass a portion of the present summer at Lucerne; but as it is Her Majesty's intention to maintain during Her stay in Switzerland, as well as on Her journey there and back, the most complete incognita, travelling under the name of Countess of Kent and declining all Royal Honours, it will be proper that you should make a communication to that effect to the Federal Authorities, and request them to make a similar communication to the Cantonal Authorities at Lucerne. It may be right to add, however, that Her Majesty's government rely on the good will of the Federal and Cantonal Authorities to provide in other respects for the comfort and freedom from molestation of the Queen during Her stay at Lucerne.
>
> Her Majesty will not require the attendance of yourself or any member of your mission at Lucerne during the whole time of Her residence at that place,

but you should be at Lucerne (in plain clothes) with any members of your mission on Her Majesty's arrival on the 7th of August, so that you may receive Her Majesty at the Railway Station and take any commands which She may see occasion to give to you.[60]

One who had high hopes of the visit was the British Consul in Geneva, who in a flowery hand wrote a despatch to Stanley:

My Lord,
   I am informed that Her Majesty the Queen intends coming to reside at Lucerne next month, that place being in my Consular district and also that Her Majesty will probably visit Geneva, on her outward, or homeward journey. I write to your Lordship, to solicit the grant of a sum of money sufficient to provide me with a Dress Uniform, in case I may require one, on any occasion during Her Majesty's stay in Switzerland.
   I may mention that I have never received anything for any outfit since my appointment, and I certainly cannot afford the expense from my private purse, already sufficiently taxed in the service of the Public since I have had the honour of holding my Consular appointment at Geneva, & for now more than 8 years.
   I hope your Lordship will consider I am making a right application on the present occasion. If I am expected, not to have anything to do with Her Majesty's visit either at Lucerne, or perhaps through this city, then I can continue to do without the Uniform – but in any case I really cannot afford myself, the expense of what, I believe amounts to some £50.0.0.[61]

This request was in vain. His Lordship not only refused point blank, but instructed the Consul to stay well away. All he got for his efforts was extra consular office work.

As the day of departure drew near, preparations went into top gear. Moving Queen Victoria's Court to Switzerland for a month occasioned a flurry of letters and telegrams between various members of the Royal Household, the Royal Mews, the Admiralty, the French authorities via the British Embassy in Paris and the Swiss authorities via the British Legation in Berne. It was a smoothly co-ordinated exercise conducted with military precision without benefit of typewriter or telephone, but with liberal use of the telegraph.

To appreciate just how modest the Queen was in her Swiss domestic requirements compared to what she was used to (and had to put up with) at home, it is enough to glance at the 1868 Royal Household List.

Part of Queen Victoria's Household in 1868. [T]here were also numbers of [hou]semaids, wardrobe maids [and] dressers (to say nothing of [Ta]ble Deckers, a Wax Fitter, [two] Coal Porters and a host of others)

Simplicity with comfort was the Queen's watchword for Lucerne, so her establishment there consisted of what, by royal standards, was a skeleton staff. Three carriages were sent out to Lucerne; one of them, on her insistence, was a particular favourite of hers, the Balmoral Sociable, specially modified for picnics, which was conveyed by ship from Aberdeen. It, together with ponies, the Queen's bed (which she mentions some years later in her Journal as having been with her in Switzerland[62]) and other paraphernalia arrived in Lucerne a few days before the Queen – an event that was duly reported not only in the local press but beyond: in Berne, readers learned from their newspaper *Der Bund* that numerous servants had brought utensils for the kitchen from England and that 'for weeks purveyors of victuals have been learning to prepare these after the manner of the English Court, for example making sandwiches in perfect cube form with butter and ham, to be enjoyed for breakfast and which are really very tasty'. The Queen also engaged one or two local maids, one of whom she took back with her to England. Then there was her trusted Highland servant John Brown, his brother Archie and three other Highlanders, as well as grooms and helpers.

During the month before leaving for Switzerland the Queen stayed at Osborne but found that the sea air brought no relief from the overpowering heatwave that was brooding over the whole country. She was counting the

Osborne House, Isle of Wight

days until her departure, but with growing trepidation. A spate of letters to the Crown Princess gives insight into the Queen's state of mind and body during these trying weeks. ' ... tho' my present life has taken a fixed form & shape & I have accepted help & comforts gratefully & feel comparative Behaglichkeit, I dislike going abroad exceedingly & wld. rather stay at home'.[63] And a week later: 'Osborne is really like Africa, quite intolerable. I wish I cld flee to some iceberg to breathe.... I fear I shall not find much cooler air in Switzerland & in that case I wish I was not going there, for it is misery to move & be active and one cld enjoy nothing. People talk of its being so hot. But it can't be worse surely than here – & at any rate the nights are cool, & that makes up for the day.'[64]

The Queen had been dreading 'the large family party at Osborne more than I can say, for I am pining for rest & quiet.'[65] Her forebodings about this month at Osborne were well-founded. The Crown Princess was told about the Queen's daughter-in-law, the Princess of Wales, and her four-day-old baby: 'Alix continues to go on quite well, but I thought she looked pale and exhausted. The baby – a mere little red lump was all I saw; & I fear the seventh grand-daughter & fourteenth grand-child becomes a very uninteresting thing – for it seems to me to go on like the rabbits in Windsor Park! The present large family party is very far from enjoyable or good for me.'[66]

The Queen then referred to what the Crown Princess had written to her (' ... nothing is better for the nerves than rising very early and having a walk before breakfast, and going early to rest – but this I think you do not like, and it does not suit you'[67]). The Queen's reaction is illuminating:

> Going to bed early & getting up early would be a total impossibility for me. The night is the only quiet time for me – & I feel able for work then & not in

the morning early. Darling Papa was very different & so are some people – but I find the greater part in this country do what I do. Walking before breakfast does not suit all – & never did me. However I shall try when I am abroad to <u>modify</u> it a little. I generally <u>now</u> breakfast at a <u>1/4 to 10</u> or <u>1/2 p. 9</u> (the <u>last</u> is what I <u>wish</u> to do – but I often can't get up early enough for that) & I generally <u>am</u> in bed by 1/2 p. 12. That is the time I <u>wish to keep to</u> – but it constantly is 1/4 to 1 & even 1 o'clock, especially when we come home late & dine late wh. is unavoidable in <u>this heat</u>.'[68]

In another letter the Queen wrote that she was suffering from an extremely obstinate 'dérangement', as she called it. 'I dare say, I shall be all the better for it tho'! – For I don't perspire & am always in a dreadful dry, burning heat & that I suppose has found its vent in this way. It is fortunate to have a few days to recover before I start on my long journey. The scenery will no doubt repay me, but I dread the whole thing a good deal.'[69] So much so that her body protested even more, as she told the Crown Princess a few days later: 'I have been very unwell this week. The Diarrhea never stopped till yesterday & then I had <u>one</u> of my most violent sick headaches with violent <u>retching</u>. I hope however I am better now, but the unusually gt. heat near the sea affects the bile & I think I shall be better for the change.'[70]

No wonder that ' ... As the time for my journey approaches, I feel nervous and anxious. Travelling <u>alone</u> without dearest Papa is a gt. trial, but Kanné arranges everything <u>so</u> well & <u>so</u> <u>quietly</u>, that he really makes it as easy <u>as possible</u>.'[71]

Her Director of Continental Journeys, J.J. Kanné, had been pressed into service alongside the indefatigable Elphinstone.

'The Queen begs Col. Elphinstone to be sure to write or to speak – to Kanné about Brienz & the Rosenlaui, for that <u>is</u> the <u>one</u> thing she <u>does</u> long to see. – The carrying up and down is not the slightest objection to her. –

She much rather <u>avoid</u> the Grindelwald.'[72]

As always, Elphinstone acted immediately. In the event, though, neither Brienz nor Rosenlaui were in fact visited during her Swiss stay – nor did the Queen explain why she preferred to avoid Grindelwald, one of Switzerland's finest and already then most popular resorts. 'The Queen thanks Col. Elphinstone very much for all his very satisfactory letters & for the explanations to Kanné. She will let Pcess Louise reconnoitre the St Gotthard & hopes it <u>may</u> be <u>effected</u>.'[73]

Arrangements had been made for a daily Messenger to ply between London and the pension in Lucerne. The Queen had told her daughter to ' ... write always either to Madame la Comtesse de Kent, Pension Wallis, Lucerne or to Gräfin v. Kent, Pension Wallis, Luzern. I travel under that name and nothing is to be directed to me – from here or elsewhere – otherwise.'[74]

Wednesday, 5 August, was *the* day. The Queen's laconic Journal entry is in surprising contrast with what must have been her state of mind, for it was on that day that she left Osborne for Switzerland.

> *August 5*
>
> *A very fine morning. – Breakfast out as usual & sitting a little while with Alice. Then took leave of her, Louis, & the 4 dear little Children, with regret. – At 1/4 p. 12 left our dear peaceful Osborne with our 3 Children, feeling sad at the parting with dear Alice. May God protect & preserve her, but I do feel a little anxious about her health. – Janie E., the Biddulphs, Col. Ponsonby, Sir William Jenner, Fräulein Bauer & Mr. Duckworth are with us.* We rowed out to the 'Victoria and Albert' & were off by 1.*

The Equerry Colonel Ponsonby portrayed what it was like on board in one of his lively and outspoken letters to his wife:

We left Osborne about half past 12. The Yacht as usual with all the Officers looking like Lord High Admirals. Molyneux and one or two others I knew but there were several new ones. Among others Lord Charles Beresford who has been appointed for his gallant conduct in saving a man's life at sea. And a Mr. Acland and a Mr. Fanshawe who had both been appointed by mistake. Fancy what idiots the Admirals must be. However they are smart looking young men tho they are not the sons of Dr. Acland or Admiral Fanshawe. I am writing in my cabin in mid channel, there is scarcely any motion – but there was just a swell about luncheon time which made Bauer turn green – but she was quickly restored by champagne. Poor Mary Bids is suffering from toothache. I persuaded her to drink wine at luncheon which got rid of it – but it has come on again. I have been in long converse with Kanné who has explained most of the arrangements at Lucerne. He thinks we return on the 5th of Sept. There is so much in the Yacht that reminds me of a passage I had in her some years ago to Antwerp, and also back again. We arrived at about 6 o'clock – A French officer came on board – and then an American from the American man of war – but that was all. The Consul, an old man with an enormous beard came also – He knew Bids and has pointed out the improvements which have taken place since you were here, which seem to be the construction of a long range of baths and nothing else. For books Jenner bagged Letters of Pliny, which he says are interesting from Osborne and I took 'Belisaire' which he says is renowned for

---

* See pages 58–9.

dulness. Jane Ely offered me some books and told me that the Correspondence of Marshal Saxe was improper. So lent me the Danvers papers which sent me to sleep. We are to land at 10 and then go on to Paris so as to arrive tomorrow morning. I believe the Q is going to be photographed and then see the Empress and thats all.[75]

The Queen's own account of the crossing is short and to the (nostalgic) point:

> ... *August 5*
> *As soon as we had passed the Needles, there was a ground swell & I had to go below, remaining there till we reached Cherbourg at 1/4p. 6. How it reminded me of the past, all seemed unaltered, & yet all is so changed for me! What used formerly to be such a delight makes me low & sad now. Dined in the deck saloon with Louise, the 2 Ladies & Ernest L. We left the yacht at 1/2p. 10, & trans-shipping on to the 'Alberta', entered the inner basin, from which we stepped on shore in the arsenal. Everything was kept quite private & a few steps took us to the train.*

This was the saloon train that the French Emperor Napoleon III had placed at the Queen's disposal for her journey to Lucerne via Paris.

LE SALON D'HONNEUR.

LA CHAMBRE A COUCHER.

The Emperor Napoleon III's saloon train

We had the Emperor's compartments, all communicating with one another & our servants near us.

IN FRANCE – EN ROUTE

Luxuriously appointed though the Emperor's train was, it rattled. The night journey from Cherbourg to Paris for a stop-over at the British Embassy with her Ambassador Lord Lyons did the Queen's jangled nerves no good at all.

Nor did things improve when she alighted in the capital, hoping perhaps for some early morning fresh air. Her Journal takes up the story.

> *August 6, Paris*
> *Could get no sleep, the carriage rocking so dreadfully. At 7 we reached Paris in a blazing heat. Ld. Lyons met us at the station, & I drove with the Children in his carriage straight to the Embassy, where I had been for a few minutes 13 years ago. Strange did it seem to me to find myself again in this great & famous capital, which I entered in such pomp & never visited but with state 13 years ago with my precious Husband & now <u>alone</u> & in such a different quiet way! Ld. Lyons took us at once upstairs, where there are fine large rooms. Had some breakfast & then washed & dressed. Afterwards sat in the garden, which is very pretty, reading & writing, till near 12, but the heat & fatigue fairly drove me in, & I remained lying quietly.*

In the afternoon the Queen put aside her newly assumed incognito for a short while in order to receive a courtesy call. It was to cost her dear.

> *... August 6*
> *at 1/2p. 3 received the Empress Eugénie, who had kindly come from Fontainebleau on purpose to see me. The Emperor is at Plombières. She remained about 10 minutes & brought 3 Ladies & 4 Gentlemen.*

Then the Queen did a terrible thing. She refused to return the Empress's call. Unroyal behaviour, a blot on Anglo-French relations that shocked France. For a Head of State a courtesy call is a solemn act symbolizing the state of relations between countries, not an empty show of social grace. In the nineteenth century, tightly governed as it was by etiquette, refusal to return a call was an even more grievous snub than it would be today. Queen Victoria had committed a gaffe of the first order and its echo was to pursue her throughout her stay in Switzerland. It was all taken very seriously, except by the Queen herself. Pleading extreme tiredness, she rested, '*overpowered by the heat*', and had some light dinner at 6, but then rather marred the effect by going on a long sightseeing drive through Paris as if nothing had happened, noting how

> *the absence of smoke makes all look bright & clean, but I regret the endless new formal building destroying all the picturesque old streets. We started at 1/2p. 7 & it was very hot in the train.*

Not many people had turned out to see the Queen go by in Paris, although there was a minor Fenian incident. However, her brief stay was in the full glare of press publicity on both sides of the Channel and expectations were high. It was obvious that the French wanted no truck with this Countess of Kent nonsense. They wanted the Queen of England. The Paris correspondent of the (London) *Court Journal* had read too much into the visit, but he reflected the mood in Paris:

> The arrival of her Majesty Queen Victoria is regarded as the great event of the season at Court, and already are gossiping speculations at work as to the purport of the visit, for no one in these days can be brought to believe that so mighty a resolve could be taken by her Britannic Majesty without some more important motive than the mere passage through Paris and the few hours' personal interview with the Empress Eugénie.'

Little did this correspondent know the Queen's condition. He went on to report rumours of a projected European summit meeting, for which this visit in Paris might have been a preparation.

> The Emperor is supposed to press urgently for a general rendezvous of the Capital Sovereigns of Europe at Darmstadt, where the prospects of the ensuing winter might be discussed. But Prussia objects to meet Bavaria, and declines *in toto* to shake hands with France. Austria would rather not sit opposite Prussia either, and Russia refuses point-blank to stand within gunshot of Austria.... The Emperor of Austria consoles himself with the reflection that he is not the only one left out of the Imperial circle. Napoleon III stands likewise looking wistfully at the merry game being played by his brother Sovereigns in which he is not invited to share, and as he walks up and down the vulgar little pasteboard promenade at Plombières, ruminates on the best and most effectual trick which he can play to disturb the enjoyment of the revellers.

In this atmosphere of political unease, with states, especially France and Prussia, eyeing one another suspiciously for signs of aggressive intent, it was only to be expected that the Queen's every move would be keenly watched for any hints as to whether Albion was favouring France or Prussia. The cynicism of the *Pall Mall Gazette*'s Paris correspondent was not wide of the mark: 'Everyone is getting tired of an armed peace which is exhausting the country, and more than one Liberal journal calls lustily for hostilities in order that tranquility may be restored.' By receiving but not returning the Empress's call, Queen Victoria kept France guessing and left the Emperor without a much-needed show of British support.

So much for the Queen's incognito on her first day abroad. Things could only improve – but in the matter of the unreturned call they did not. The Foreign Secretary, Lord Stanley, arrived in Paris in the evening en route for Lucerne 'by the common train'[76] as he put it, and was briefed by the Embassy after Lord Lyons had seen the Queen off in Napoleon III's saloon train. 'They said the Queen's visit had gone off well,' he noted in his diary, 'but were evidently vexed at her refusing to call on the Empress.... It is no doubt a mere form, and there was the excuse of want of time, but it is just on these points that the Imperial Court, as being parvenu, is touchy.'[77] Stanley wrote in similar vein to Disraeli: ' ... the only contre-temps was the great Lady's absolute refusal to return the Empress's call, which as a matter of ceremony she ought.'[78]

But it soon became clear that the French were taking it as more than a trivial slight. Stanley called on the French Foreign Minister Moustier and General Fleury of the Imperial Court, whom he found 'deeply mortified at the Queen's incivility to the Empress (it is nothing less): he could not help alluding to it more than once, though very civilly.'[79]

This is more than could be said of the French press, ever on the lookout for knocking copy about the British. Stanley sent Disraeli the mildest of the articles, in *Figaro*, which he thought would amuse him.

The Queen of England in Paris

Hardly had her Majesty Queen Victoria arrived at the Embassy yesterday than she dismissed her suite and remained alone. She retired to her simply decorated, austere room and rested until lunch. Lunch was taken en famille, not even Lord Lyons being invited to the Royal table ...

After lunch Her Majesty walked in the garden, seated herself there and spent at least one and a half hours reading the philosophical and religious works of the Prince Consort.

The Queen was fatigued. Prey to extremely painful attacks of neuralgia since the death of Prince Albert, travelling causes her great discomfort and she cannot undertake journeys of any length with impunity.

Her accompanying physician Dr Jenner, who has prescribed complete rest and the sojourn in Switzerland, yesterday interposed with the Royal traveller to abstain from excitement and observe absolute calm.

So she spent the entire afternoon in complete isolation without the slightest distraction, in the Embassy garden. The Queen was still in her travelling clothes and in place of a day bonnet wore a cap recalling those of Mary Stuart.

In the meantime, the Empress had arrived at the Tuileries from Fontainebleau.... After lunch, in other words about half past two, her Majesty the Empress, wearing a mauve tulle dress with a matching hat topped by a spray of trembling osprey feathers, set out with her retinue in two-horse ceremonial carriages to the Elysée from whence she would visit the Queen at half past three.

Queen Victoria hurried through the drawing-rooms, arriving below the vestibule and descended the staircase to meet the Empress whom she embraced with a show of great friendship and effusion. The Empress, having presented her retinue in one of the first morning-rooms, left them with the persons accompanying the Queen and with Lord Lyons. Their Majesties, separated from all these people by a morning-room, retired to an official drawing-room next to the magnificent Throne Room and spent twenty minutes in conversation. The Queen, while escorting the Empress back, expressed her sincere regrets that owing to her fatigue and indisposition she was unable to receive the Empress in the manner she would have wished.

The Queen greeted the members of the Empress's suite, accompanied the Empress to the foot of the peristyle and embraced her once again. The Empress then took her leave and departed to the Elysée.

For an hour and ten minutes the Empress and a crowd of onlookers waited in vain, exposed to the elements, for the Queen's return visit. The crowd murmured its dissatisfaction and manifested its sympathy in favour of the Empress. Finally, no longer able to count on the return visit of her sister-in-royalty, the Empress requested Mesdames Paulet and Jacquot to disrobe her, the ceremonial carriages were dismissed and at five minutes past five the Empress and her suite left the Elysée in open carriages for the Gare de Lyon and Fontainebleau.

This incident of considerable importance preoccupied the crowd which, in interpreting the apparent refusal to return the visit, evidently misjudged the reasons which had prevented Her Majesty Queen Victoria from returning the call. But public sentiment neither reasons nor comprehends: the crowd was dissatisfied and on her departure the Empress was the recipient of the acclaim which was a consequence of the public frame of mind.

Let us say that at the Embassy there was surprise at the Queen's eschewing a return visit and she was earnestly requested to do so. But as loyal chronicler we should add that the Queen was so exhausted and prostrated by fatigue and suffering that her indisputable goodwill was vanquished by the circumstances.

This was not the end of the story.

THE QUEEN IN SWITZERLAND

On the morning the Queen arrived in Switzerland, *The Times* in its main leading article came out with a veritable hymn of praise on the glories of Switzerland and on how fortunate the Sovereign was to be allowed at last to revel in them. The last paragraph contains a plea that would no doubt strike a chord with many a plagued twentieth-century Royal.

LONDON. FRIDAY, AUGUST 7, 1868

In a rapid journey HER MAJESTY has crossed the Channel to Cherbourg, gone by train to Paris, and thence proceeds by way of Troyes and Bâle to the Lake of Lucerne, where the Royal party are expected to arrive this morning. Every one will be disposed to congratulate HER MAJESTY on having chosen so noble a region as Switzerland for her autumn tour and on making so beautiful a spot as Lucerne her first residence. To a large proportion of the QUEEN's subjects the Swiss mountains are not new, though they can never grow old. Every year hundreds of English people of all ages pass over certain well-known tracks, and delight their eyes with the sight of the most magnificent natural objects which Europe can boast. The most frequented spots, the most hackneyed routes, present the most glorious forms of mountain, lake, or waterfall; for the places are visited and, it may be, vulgarized in direct proportion to their beauty and their fame. Thus, the least adventurous of the travelling public – the 'procession of cockneys' – are acquainted with regions whose names are household words wherever there is any feeling for grandeur and sublimity. But it is the ill fortune of Royalty to be less free in its movements than the meanest of its subjects. The middle-class family which can spare a very moderate sum has its way made every year smoother for its Swiss tour. The railways south of the Thames once passed, it finds comfortable travelling at reasonable rates, and hotels where the food is made palatable and where it is possible to drink the wine. No wonder that the attractions of fine scenery, new and more lively modes of life, with the comforts of good accommodation offered by people who thoroughly understand the business of entertainment, should attract the QUEEN's subjects, and it seems almost a pity that exalted dignity or public duties should forbid the highest personages in the world to share these pleasures. But certain it is that even now Monarchs are very much restricted, or, in obedience to custom, have very much restricted themselves from visiting foreign parts. The younger branches of the reigning Houses do, indeed, see the world, though even they must go with a certain kind of State, and must be worried almost to death by the pertinacious curiosity of the crowd, particularly of genteel English. The Crowned Head must as a general rule be content to bear its weight of dignity in its own land. The tradition is against the locomotion of Sovereigns, and it will take many years before it dies out. The political relations of States, and the significance which rumour attaches to many Royal movements, tend to keep Sovereigns at home, since, though they may avoid ceremonial receptions by the use of an *incognito*, they cannot throw off their identity nor attain perfect privacy and irresponsibility. However visionary may be some of the drawbacks to the happiness of Monarchs which moralists profess to discover, there can be no doubt that they are deprived to a certain extent of free intercourse with the world, the free gratification of curiosity, and pursuit of adventure.

It must be remembered, then, that the QUEEN now, for the first time, goes among the Alps. For the first time she will see the transcendent beauties of the Lake of the Four Cantons, the Righi and Pilatus, with the distant mountain ranges which shut in the view; for the first time she will explore those shores where every turn discloses something grand and rare, unparalleled, at least, in these regions of the globe. How much the QUEEN feels the charm of mountain scenery those who have read her Journals in the Highlands need not be told. Her surprise and delight at the objects which she met in those northern tours are expressed with the utmost simplicity and sincerity. If, then, the brown hills of Scotland affected her with such emotion, what must be her pleasure in looking for the first time on the mighty masses of the Alps, with their clothing of snow and glacier, their waterfalls, their pine forests, and all those natural features which once seen are never forgotten! We sincerely hope that the QUEEN will have strength and spirits to see a good deal of Switzerland. Such a foreign excursion is likely more than anything else to give strength to the body and elasticity to the mind, to remove the depression caused by long-continued sorrow, and to make the sufferer take a new and brighter view of life. There can be no doubt that one of the best remedies even for bodily ailments is change of scene, and the meeting with entirely new objects, both living and inanimate. The benefit which doctors often attribute to what is called 'change of air' is more often caused by a break up of the monotony of ideas, and is a moral rather than a physical influence. In Switzerland it is difficult to say which is the more new and strange, the aspect of nature or the human life which accompanies and has grown out of it, and to one who has not been much abroad we can well imagine that a month in this most beautiful of European regions would produce a more beneficial effect than any number of changes of place between one point of Great Britain and another.

As the 'Countess of KENT' travels for the benefit of her health, and for that reason dispenses with the courtesies which foreign authorities would offer, we hope that English tourists will respect the privacy of the Royal party. Loyalty is no doubt a very excellent sentiment, but it can be cherished without invading its exalted object at every turn of her daily walks; nor has it, indeed, any real connexion with that vulgar curiosity which makes a well-dressed English mob rush after a Prince as if he were some extraordinary animal, exhibited for the first time. It is not unnecessary to make these remarks, since the fact that the QUEEN is at Lucerne, and that only well-to-do English people are likely to be found there, may be no protection to her; for, unhappily, respectable people are the greatest offenders in this respect. The QUEEN has gone on a tour which we all hope will be a pleasant one; let all assist in making it so, by abstaining from importunate loyalty. Sovereigns seldom have the opportunity

The Queen's Suite at Lucerne

Princess Louise, Queen Victoria's fourth daughter, aged 20

Prince Leopold (*left*) and Prince Arthur (*right*), Queen Victoria's fourth and third sons, aged 15 and 18

Princess Beatrice, Queen Victoria's fifth daughter and youngest child, aged 11

The Hon. Lady Biddulph, Hon. Bedchamber Woman (wife of Sir Thomas)

Revd J.R. Duckworth, Prince Leopold's Governor

· *Incognita* ·

The Queen's Suite at Lucerne

Colonel Henry Ponsonby, Equerry to Queen Victoria

Jane, Marchioness of Ely, Lady of the Bedchamber

Sir Thomas Biddulph, Keeper of the Privy Purse

Sir William Jenner, Bart., MD., Physician-in-Ordinary to Queen Victoria

Fräulein Ottilie Bauer, Princess Beatrice's Governess

of laying aside their majesty with their Crown and Robes; on these rare occasions, then, let them have the agreeable freedom of a lower station.

The Queen was accompanied in Switzerland by a few particularly congenial members of her Household.

The party also numbered five Highlanders, including the stalwart Highland Servant John Brown and his brother Archie, resplendent in their kilts but, surprisingly, attracting little attention. Hovering in the background were her Continental courier J.J. Kanné and the Swiss guide A. Hofmann, who had earned his spurs for his guiding of Prince Arthur and Elphinstone's 1864 Swiss tour.

Queen Victoria, 1868.
'Of late years, especially since the sad loss of her husband, Queen Victoria has undergone a great change, both in mind and body. The charm of her presence always rose more from the natural expression of an amiable disposition than from any regularity of feature or grace of manner. Her eyes are blue and bright, her hair dark, and her complexion is now somewhat sallow. It is marked by deep lines of affliction, and yet those do not make her expression less attractive. In the approaches of age she has gained that which may be called the beauty of goodness.'
From *Sketches and Anecdotes of Her Majesty the Queen, the late Prince Consort, and other members of the Royal Family*, selected and arranged by J.G. Hodgins (Sampson Low, 1868)

PART Two

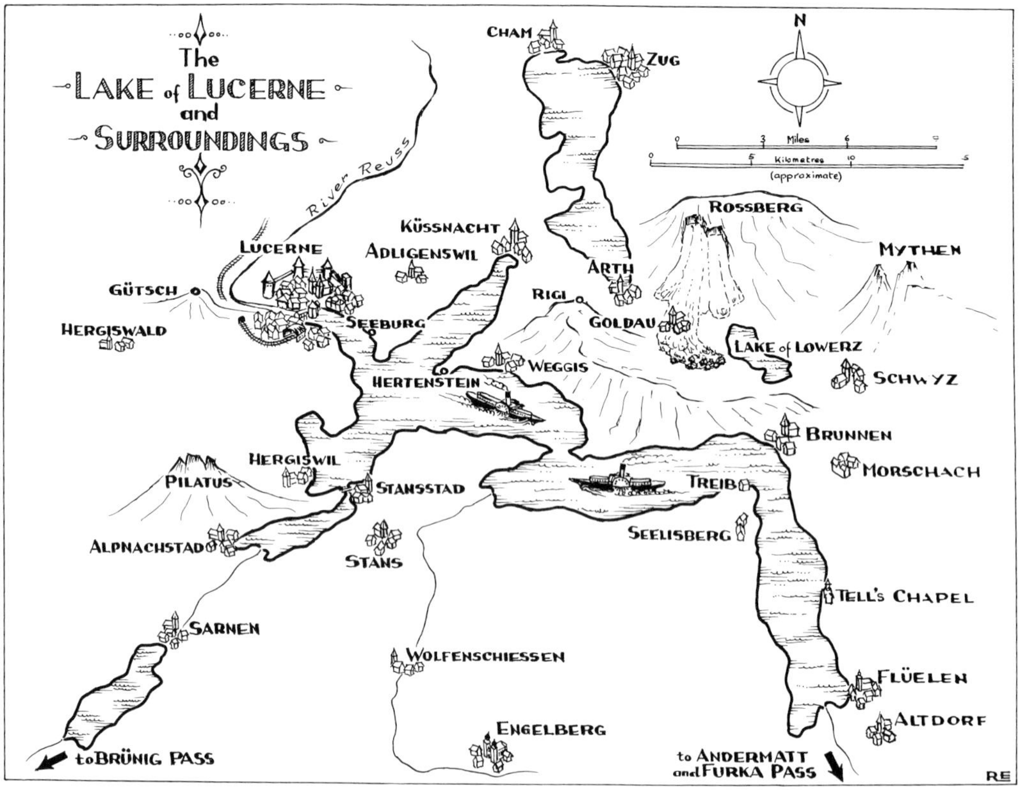
The
LAKE of LUCERNE
and
SURROUNDINGS
N
Miles
0
3
6
9
Kilometres
0
5
10
15
(approximate)
River Reuss
CHAM
ZUG
ROSSBERG
MYTHEN
KÜSSNACHT
ADLIGENSWIL
LUCERNE
GÜTSCH
HERGISWALD
SEEBURG
ARTH
RIGI
GOLDAU
LAKE of LOWERZ
SCHWYZ
HERTENSTEIN
WEGGIS
BRUNNEN
MORSCHACH
HERGISWIL
PILATUS
STANSSTAD
TREIB
SEELISBERG
ALPNACHSTAD
STANS
TELL'S CHAPEL
SARNEN
WOLFENSCHIESSEN
FLÜELEN
ALTDORF
ENGELBERG
to BRÜNIG PASS
to ANDERMATT
and FURKA PASS
RE

3 Haven

After a second night on the train, this time not quite so sleepless, Queen Victoria steamed across the north-west frontier of Switzerland and into Basle at seven o'clock. Breakfast was brought into the saloon and they were soon off again on the way to their destination, Lucerne.

The Queen's Journal entry for this first Swiss day is long and detailed, her pen stimulated by new surroundings and by the triumph of having at last reached the haven she had dreamed of all these years. She begins with an account of the journey from Basle to Lucerne:

August 7
From here the scenery is lovely, though unfortunately one does not see any of the highest hills. All looked so fresh & green. We passed the valley of the Birs, celebrated for a gallant defence of the Swiss in the 15th century. Our next stop was at Sissach, after which comes a longish tunnel & an immense one 5 minutes long, after Laufelfingen. During the making of it 50 men were buried alive.

The Emperor Napoleon III's saloon train

Tunnelling technique was in its infancy when this, Switzerland's longest tunnel at the time, was built in the 1850s. Hence the accident.

63

The upper Hauenstein tunnel, then Switzerland's longest, at its opening in 1858

What the Queen does not mention in her Journal is that the tunnel, and indeed the whole line, was designed and built by British engineers. This omission says much about the predominant British image of Switzerland, which had undergone a sea-change during the nineteenth century. Whereas before that time attention had been focused on the cities, on politics, religion, trade and industry and intellectual life, the focus shifted with the awakening of enthusiasm for the beauties and excitement of the Alps in the eighteenth century. The magnetic attraction of the mountains became so strong that by the time of Queen Victoria's visit Switzerland meant lakeside and mountain resorts to holiday in, with perhaps only a night or two spent in a city to see the sights and with villages as a picturesque contrast.

Yet relations between the two countries had for centuries been many-sided, close and as time went on increasingly cordial. The Swiss played no small part in British public life, and Switzerland underwent an industrial revolution that paralleled or followed British lines, often adapting British technology and methods. Much British investment and know-how went into the development of the country's rail network. There were even wild flights of fancy such as a project for a direct line between the Suez Canal and Denmark. If Queen Victoria had known that the line she was travelling on was British-owned, and that the tunnel was an early engineering marvel brought about by her subject Thomas Brassey (without benefit of powerful machinery), she would surely have at least mentioned this, and Princess Beatrice – a dutiful daughter to the last – would have copied it.

More likely she was never told. It would have been an unromantic irrelevance, as remote from her present purpose as was any thought about, say, the Anglo-Swiss trade treaty of twelve years earlier. Or indeed her own urgent intercession on behalf of Switzerland in 1857, when Prussia had mobilized and was marching on the Swiss in order to reinforce their claim to Neuchâtel, a Prussian Principality which had recently declared for membership of the Swiss Confederation. Later, as she sailed on the Lake of Lucerne in her chartered ship, she never knew – or if she did, she did not think it worth mentioning – that another steamer plying the lake had been built in England and brought overland from Basle to Lucerne.

She was coming to Switzerland to get away from it all, and one can almost sense Queen Victoria's impatience to put the world behind her from the way she continues her account of that first day in Switzerland.

> ... August 7
> We stopped for the last time at Alten,* the central station for all the Swiss railways. Passed the Lake of Sempach, extremely lovely & blue, with wooded banks, & then began the most glorious scenery, mountain peaks, towering one above the other in the most wonderful way, till we at length came close on Lucerne, passing the splendid emerald green coloured river of the Reuss. My own dear Scotch sociable was at the station, driven from the box with 4 horses by a local coachman, & I entered into it with the Children. Kanné sat on the box & Brown behind.

'You may like to know *how* we go about. Almost always in a (Scotch) Sociable, the guide Hofmann sitting on the box with the Coachman, a safe but dreadfully slow man who drives 4 in hand, & Brown in a dickey behind wh. has purposely been added & under wh. is a box wh. I have to all my Sociables these last 2 years, in wh. goes the luncheon & tea baskets &c. Sometimes, but for short drives, I also use my Waggonette, & then no guide goes.'
(From Queen Victoria's letter to her daughter, Crown Princess Victoria, 19 August 1868)

For weeks the press on the Continent had been relaying speculation, then confirmation of the Queen's forthcoming visit to Switzerland. The arrival of her horses, carriages and baggage at Lucerne a few days ahead of her had also been duly noted in the Swiss press. Now, as she herself stepped out of the train at Lucerne and looked around anxiously, she will have been greatly relieved to find that her incognito was doing its work: the Swiss Federal authorities and local officials had taken the hint and were staying away.

* Alten/Olten.

Not so the public. The local press reported that the Lucerne police, in full strength and gala uniform, had difficulty in keeping the eager crowd at a respectable distance. The Queen was described as 'a woman of about 50, not tall, fairly corpulent, with a red face and clad in mourning for her departed husband'.

The Queen's account of the day continues with mounting enthusiasm.

> ... *August 7*
> *Drove through a small part of the town, which is most picturesquely situated, up to our house, called Pension Wallis. The drive up was very hot, & took about 1/2 an hour from the station. Not many people out & no authorities. The view from the house & above all from my sitting-room window, overlooking the Lake with the town in front, skirted by the most glorious mountains, & brilliant verdure in the foreground, is something ideal. Really it was like what I had dreamt of, but could hardly believe to see in reality! How much dearest Albert wished I should see Switzerland, <u>how</u> he admired it, & how everything beautiful makes me think of <u>him</u>! The small house is very snug & comfortable & felt very cool, & there is room for all of us, excepting the*

Pension Wallis. On the left, the '*Châlet quite adjoining*' mentioned in the Journal

Biddulphs & Col. Ponsonby, who live in a Châlet quite adjoining. Had some breakfast directly after we arrived, & then washed, dressed & rested. Luncheon was at 2 in a good sized Diningroom.

View of Lucerne and surroundings from the Gütsch. (Oil painting by J.J. Zelger, 1868, commissioned by Queen Victoria)

… August 7
Again resting. – At 1/4 to 6 took a drive with the 2 Ladies, the Guide Hofmann, sitting on the box with the coachman & Brown behind on the rumble. We went through a fine wood of all kinds of trees, on emerging from which one suddenly came upon Pilatus 7,300 ft. high, on the highest peaks & summits of which are very pointed rocks. The whole was glowing in the setting sun, what is called here 'Alpenglühen'. It was glorious & the evening pleasantly cool. We passed most picturesque châlets, with galleries, many overhung with vines. It looks so pretty to see them dotted about the hills. The Rigi, 5,910 ft., one has constantly before one. The vegetation nearly goes to the top of it & one can plainly see the Hotel at the top. Home through the town, a little before 8, quite delighted with our 1st drive. – The 2 Ladies, Sir Thomas, Col. Ponsonby & Sir Wm. Jenner dined with us. Afterwards we sat out, looking at the town below.

Later Lady Ely will have slipped away quietly to write the first of the private letters that the Prime Minister had requested of her. In order to keep an eye on the Queen at long range, Disraeli had an impressive intelligence-gathering network: the Queen herself, not at her prodigious best as a correspondent while in Switzerland, but still keeping up a steady flow of black-rimmed memos and letters, with her opinions on affairs of state such as the appointment of Church dignitaries and with accounts of her activities; then the Foreign Secretary Lord Stanley, Ponsonby, Biddulph, the press, and, as on this first day, Jane Ely. After giving a detailed account of the day and hoping that the Queen would like the place ('it is most private'),[80] she loyally and with monumental understatement took the Queen's side on the great Issue of the Unreturned Call in Paris: 'The Queen felt too tired to return Her Imperial Majesty's visit, which was rather a disappointment, I believe.' The letter ends on an emollient note: 'The Queen told me, the other evening, you suited her so well & understood Her Majesty, which was a great comfort to her & you were so sensible & kind, the Queen said.'[81]

The following morning the Queen awoke refreshed.

> *August 8*
> *Very hot, but I slept without moving, & the beauty of the morning was very great & a feast for the eye. We 4 breakfasted together, in a charming spot, in the shade, near the house, & I sat & wrote in a little summer house close to the stables, till near 1. The air was very pleasant, though the sun scorching.*

One of the letters the Queen wrote that morning was to her eldest daughter Victoria, Crown Princess of Prussia:

What am I to say of the glorious scenery in Switzerland; the view from this Hse wh. is <u>vy high</u> is most wonderfully beautiful with the Lake – Pilatus, the Righi &c – & I can <u>hardly</u> believe my eyes – when I look at it! It seems like a painting or decoration – a <u>dream!</u> –

We took a charming drive last night round below Pilatus by Krienz – & the evng. lights – the beautiful woods & <u>all</u> so green & fresh (whereas with us all is parched & burnt) was <u>quite</u> too delightful. It was cool & pleasant. The heat of the sun is fearful but the air is so pure & light it refreshes one. I am sitting writing in a vy pretty little Summer House – near the House – wh. is shady & fr. wh. you have lovely <u>peeps</u>....

I hope to take a fine drive this afternoon to get a <u>sight</u> of the Glaciers & Jungfrau. Now goodbye & God bless you.[82]

Watercolour of the same view, by Princess Louise, 8 August 1868

'After luncheon sketching the heavenly view from my window. All the highest hills could be seen, reaching up to the very clouds!' (Journal, 8 August 1868) Watercolour by Queen Victoria, 8 August 1868

Later that afternoon the Queen and her two daughters went on their first drive through Lucerne and along the lake, taking their tea with them, *'lost in admiration of all we saw, & which is so difficult to describe'*.[83] They returned at eight, the Queen remarking that it was still very hot.

The weather was also the first thing she noticed the next morning, a Sunday:

9 August
Most dreadfully hot. – Breakfast out at 9 & sat out writing, until we had service at 12, performed by Mr Duckworth in the Diningroom.

Such services were being held all over Switzerland, which – as a German tourist remarked – was a free country occupied by the British. With colonizing zeal and religious fervour they were building their own churches all over the place, even in the mountain hamlet Arolla at 6,500 feet altitude; where there were no English, Scottish or local churches to use, the public rooms of hotels would be pressed into Anglican service. Not everybody appreciated this, including the author Samuel Butler who, touring Switzerland in 1869, wrote: 'As much as possible I keep away from English-frequented hotels in Italy and Switzerland because I find that if I do not go to service on Sunday I am made uncomfortable. It is this bullying that I want to do away with.'[84]

An afternoon drive took the Queen along the Emmental with fruit trees, houses and *'through such a picturesque small village, with a Church & Convent & as one wound up the hill, one could hear the bells ringing for Vespers. Got out & took our tea, which was most refreshing, under a tree.'*

The Queen had come to Switzerland for a complete change – but there were limits. Never once during all her stay did she miss out on her afternoon tea. This was no mean achievement: there tended to be an absence of tea-making infrastructure on mountains and glaciers, apart from which the Swiss have never been great tea-drinkers. But, as we shall see, Victorian ingenuity invariably prevailed; neither did the Queen complain on the very rare occasions when she had to wait until 6 o'clock.

> *... August 9*
> *After passing the Emmenbrücke, the whole range of mountains, surmounted by glaciers & snow-topped ones with the Titlis, 13,000 ft. high, could be beautifully & clearly seen, all glowing with that pink hue, which lasts but a very short time. – Dined outside, & remained sitting out till 1/2p. 10.*

The Queen's first week in her Lucerne hideaway settled down into a sedate routine of walks, rides, drives and long periods in the garden, resting, writing or painting. She liked her early morning rides on her pony Flora in the *'deliciously cool'* fir wood nearby, although Flora was *'frantic with the horse flies, which pursue man & beast here!'*[85]

Unfortunately there were annoyances: the press reported that the Queen had taken exception to the peace of the Sabbath being disturbed by the noise of bowling coming from a nearby public garden ('the perpetual thunder of these Royal Salutes', as the *Court Journal* put it) and that she had offered the princely sum of 2,000 francs (£80 at the exchange rate of that time, 25 francs to the £) to stop the sport on Sundays – but to no avail.

There were a few excursions on the lake. The first one stimulated the Queen into making four sketches from the steamer *Winkelried*, kept at her

Pension Wallis: the Queen's drawing room (*left*) and the Queen's bedchamber (*right*)

The steamer *Winkelried*, used by the Queen during her stay

disposal during her whole stay. Carriages would be taken on board so that part of an excursion could be made by road, picking up the steamer again at another point.

August 11
The air seemed fresher, when we were out at breakfast, but whilst I was sitting out, it got much hotter again.... At 12 started with Louise, Janie E. & Sir T. Biddulph, driving down to where a steamer was waiting for us. Embarked taking our carriage on board with us & steamed off at once. Pleasant air & most splendid views as we went along. Hofmann explained every place we passed. We came to Tell's Chapel, under which

William Tell's Chapel on the shores of Lake Lucerne, near Flüelen

we stopped for a while. The height of the mountains & rocks here is stupendous & we were told chamois were to be found.... Truly glorious was the view, as we approached Fluellen, the Urirothstock, with snow, rising splendidly above it, & lower down richly wooded mountains, made a most beautiful picture. We lay quite close enough to Tell's Chapel, which is open in front, to see the curious old fresco paintings on the wall, representing incidents in his life. Here it was that he jumped out of the boat & was saved in the midst of a storm. Had our luncheon on board the steamer. The Lake a most marvellous sapphire blue and emerald green colour, changing from one to the other. Luncheon over, we went on to Fluellen, where we disembarked, our carriage being easily unshipped & at once drove off through the very picturesque town built up against the mountain. Drove some time along the Lake, on the celebrated Axenstrasse, hewn through the rock with many tunnels. The heat was unfortunately so great, that I could hardly enjoy it. Stopped in a shady place to take our tea, & went on to Brunnen, where we again got on board the steamer. Only a few people had assembled at the pier. The great composer Wagner's Villa, not far from Lucerne, was pointed out to us. Got home at 1/2 p. 7. Heavy clouds had gathered & a thunderstorm broke forth, continuing with violent rain for 2 hours. The echo in the mountains makes the thunder seem very loud.

Tunnel on Axenstrasse

The Queen wrote to her eldest daughter Princess Victoria about this first excursion:

> … It was most splendid & nothing can exceed the beauty of the Lake in any direction. The view up to Weggis – to Brunnen & Fluelen – with those splendid peaked mountains all wooded & the Urirothstock in the midst is really <u>quite overwhelming</u>. Then on to Stanzstadt … with the splendid Pilatus overhanging the Lake to the right – & the Lake itself, that wonderful colour – varying from saphire blue to emerald green – is too glorious![86]

The Equerry Colonel Ponsonby gave a lively account of the previous evening at the pension in a letter home to his wife. Some of the Queen's suite had taken an exploratory trip on the steamer that afternoon:

> At 4 Louise Leopold Duckworth Bauer Bids & J. Ely & I went to Lucerne to our steamer which was in waiting. Most luxurious with chairs etc., and we have tea on board. We went up to the other end of the lake and visited Tells Chapel & then back only just in time for dinner. The Queen with Mary Bids had been driven in by a thunder storm. Discourse at dinner about William Tell. I'm sure says the Queen if there is any doubt about his existence Colonel Ponsonby don't believe in him. 'Well Mum it is curious there is a similar tale told of one

Toko of Denmark.' Whereupon Bids split into instant clatter of laughter. I got this from 'Myths of the Middle Ages'. Toko was 300 years before Tell. Jenner horrified 'But you don't believe in Toko?' Of course I hadn't expressed such opinion but being then pressed I denied all belief in Tell and Toko and said the story was a very old Indian one. Jenner indignant. Murray says Tells chapel was built by 114 people who personally knew Tell. Louise says that Froude says these 114 people are myths as much as Tell.... Kanné tells me that Mr Brown and Dr. Jenner will drive him mad. J.B.* of course asks for everything for the Queen as if he were in Windsor Castle, and if anything cannot be got he says it must – and it is. Jenner who has never seen foreign L.† before runs about to each in a state of high disgust and says they must be entirely altered – Jenner is right of course – but he rather over estimates the idea of bad smells, because perched up here there are not except in one or two places.[87]

Dining room of the Pension Wallis and Princess Louise's sketch of Sir Thomas Biddulph ('Bids' or 'Father Jim')

Although the Pension Wallis was almost new, an entry in the Lord Chamberlain's 'Statement of Her Majesty's expenses on Tour in Switzerland' shows that to fit it for Royal occupation a goodly sum was spent on the local purchase of furniture, carpets, baths and sundries, glass, china, looking-glasses, a telegraphic apparatus and, to put Jenner's mind at rest, a prodigious amount of cleanser for the patent WC. The total came to £407.0.1 – a lot of

* John Brown.
† i.e. lavatories.

· *Haven* ·

money in those days, but not extravagant; by comparison, as much as half that amount had been spent for entertainment during one evening a month earlier, on the occasion of one of the rare State Balls at Buckingham Palace, for the hire of marquees and tents and the attendance of Mr. Dan Godfrey's Quadrille Band (Mr. D. Godfrey and 36 Performers).[88]

Jenner's fears on the score of Swiss sanitation were unfounded. Neither the Queen nor any of her entourage caught anything untoward. On the contrary, the Queen was on the mend and venturing further afield. A drive around Lucerne elicited a Journal entry about the Lion Monument:

Lion monument, Lucerne

August 12
Drove up to see the Lion Monument put up to the memory of Louis XVI's poor Swiss Guard, who were all killed in the Revolution of the 10th of Aug. 1793.[*] *Got out & went close up to look at it. It is most*

---

[*] In fact it was in 1792 that the Swiss Guard were killed, defending Marie Antoinette during the storming of the Tuileries.

striking, grand & touching. The lion is hewn in bas relief, out of the rock, represented lying pierced & dying, grasping with his paws a shield on which are the Fleurs de Lis of the Bourbons.

... August 12
Stopped to take our tea in the carriage ... Our very slow but safe coachman drove beautifully through the very narrow streets & round the sharp corners.

The Queen was obviously relishing her new-found freedom. But she was, after all, the Head of State and was not let off the hook completely. The umbilical cord with London was never broken, although Disraeli knew what was good for him and made sure his sovereign was bothered as little as possible. In any case, with Parliament in recess and the summer holiday season in full swing, there was no great political activity. Messengers arrived, but especially at first the Queen was in no way overworked. During this first week, for example, Sir Thomas Biddulph wrote on her behalf to Disraeli, conveying her approval of some Ministerial appointments, and adding for good measure: 'There is no inconvenience from Tourists or Inhabitants, who behave very well.'[89]

The Foreign Secretary Lord Stanley was also under-employed at the time. He was on hand to take care of any foreign or other affairs that might blow up. Kept at arm's length by the Queen and staying in a Lucerne hotel, he was having a hugely enjoyable – and very energetic – holiday, with very few calls on his time to distract him from his marathon 'rambles',[90] as he called them. These kept him happily occupied for many hours every day, whereas it took him only a few minutes to deal with the correspondence brought by the messengers. During his first week his royal duties consisted of nothing more onerous than fending off some people who wanted to call on the Queen. Among these was a Dutch aide-de-camp, sent by the King of Holland to pay his respects to the Queen, and even the Papal Nuncio in Berne, who had hoped that he could personally convey the Pope's good wishes.

The British diplomatic staff in Berne called on Stanley but did not get near the Queen. In his diary Stanley records a thumb-nail sketch of the Swiss, given to him by the Minister, John Savile Lumley, the head of the Legation:

Lumley talks about the people, praises them highly, says their politics are very pure, their offices miserably paid, but they continue to get capable men to fill them: there is really, and not only in name, an open career: one of their leading politicians in his youth helped his father who kept a small cabaret: and such cases are not rare. There are no very rich people, fortunes in general are moderate: but pauperism is unknown. They work hard, and in addition to their farms, follow some trade or other occupation which keeps them from idleness in the winter. They have moreover the exceptional advantage of having perhaps a million sterling brought yearly into the country by foreigners.[91]

Very likely the Queen kept well away from such unholiday-like conversation, in line with her policy of having a complete change and keeping her involvement in affairs of state to an irreducible minimum. By now, the end of her first week in Lucerne, she was well ensconced in her quarters on the hill, she had got her bearings and was chafing at the bit to go further afield.

It was not to be.

4 Frustration

As the days wore on Queen Victoria became more and more aware that there was something seriously wrong – and getting worse by the day.

Nature had set the Queen's thermostat at a sub-Arctic comfort level: she felt well at Balmoral, for example, while others shivered, but found 'normal' temperatures unpleasantly hot, and real heat unbearable. One of her aims in choosing Switzerland for this holiday had always been to find 'bracing air',[92] and this expectation grew during the summer of 1868 as England baked in the fiercest heatwave for decades.

The journey to Switzerland had not been easy, with Paris *'in a blazing heat'*[93] already at 7 a.m. after a sleepless night in a rocking train, followed by another night in the *'very hot'*[94] train to Basle. But the first day in Switzerland had made up for it all, and she found the evening pleasantly cool.

The rest of her first week was hot by any standards. In fact, the Queen had got away from the English heatwave only to walk straight into an almighty one in Switzerland. It was Queen's weather with a vengeance. The Swiss had been having a cool summer; promptly upon her arrival the greatest and longest heatwave in living memory set in – and broke just after she left. Not quite what the doctor ordered ...

The Queen felt the heat, of course, but at first there was much to distract her from it: exhilaration over her new surroundings, the glory of the scenery and relief at having successfully managed her great escape. But by mid-August, the beginning of her second week, when the novelty had worn off and the mountains beckoned, the heat was really getting to her. And not only the heat, but a phenomenon called Föhn, an ill wind brought about by the meeting of cold and warm air over the Alps, with associated abrupt changes in air pressure.

People react very differently to Föhn: some do not even notice it, some have minor symptoms such as light-headedness which they shrug off, others get leaden feet and violent headaches. Queen Victoria was clearly susceptible. It says much for her determination of spirit that she battled against the symptoms and got on with her holiday, even though the weather was putting paid to the Alpine expeditions she yearned for. Central Switzerland during that second week of the Queen's stay was plagued not only by Föhn but by recurring thunderstorms and showers that made the air oppressively damp

· *Frustration* ·

and shrouded the mountains in mist. Not very amusing.

Her Journal entries for these days are mostly laconic about her feelings, referring only to headaches and heavy air. But she was more outspoken in her letters to her eldest daughter Victoria. At the beginning of this trying week she was still putting a brave face on it:

> I believe it is quite exceptional here to have such dreadful heat <u>all</u> day with <u>hot</u> nights. Yesterday was better after another dreadful thunderstorm on Thursday Evng. & pouring rain. But today it is again very hot tho there is a pleasant air. It prevents my undertaking <u>any</u> lengthened expeditions for the day – or riding or walking wh. is <u>vy provoking</u>. – I have had some very pleasant & beautiful afternoon drives – quietly & peaceably from 5 to 8 – or a little before. – We breakfast out about 9 & then I sit out writing – in the shade, but more I cannot do in the heat. This will show you how <u>far</u>, how <u>very far</u> from well, poor, old Mama is – & it depresses & discourages me. <u>Home</u>, at least Scotland, is the <u>best</u> place for <u>me</u> for my health, <u>that I feel</u>. Perhaps (if I live) in some years I may be better. It is God's Will & whatever He sends – sorrow, or joy, or suffering, or comfort must <u>all</u> be borne with meek submission and gratitude! – Still, for all that, I am very glad I am here & can see God's most <u>glorious</u> Creation – as I am sure it can <u>no</u> <u>where</u> be surpassed.[95]

Below the Schwarzenberg. Watercolour by Queen Victoria, 16 August 1868

The Foreign Secretary, Lord Stanley, was invited up to the Pension Wallis and noted in his diary that he saw the Queen afterwards: '... she in good spirits, and pleased with the place, but complains of heat, and Jenner says it is too much for her, and almost makes her ill ... I thought her in good humour, which is by no means always the case.'[96] To the Prime Minister Stanley wrote: 'The great lady keeps herself very close: I saw her last Sunday in excellent looks and high good humour: she said little of public affairs, but what she did say was to blame the opposition, and express decided sympathy with her ministers. She hoped the elections would go well. She seems to pass her time chiefly sitting in her garden, and driving out in the evening at a tremendous pace ... We have had great heat for some days, which she suffered from (and indeed it was such as I have never felt in Europe) ...'[97]

The Queen, never one to suffer silently for long, soon gave full vent to her frustration, and on 19 August she wrote to Princess Victoria:

This climate is dreadful ... so damp & clammy when it is not boiling – & I get dreadfully tired & have constant headaches & little appetite. Beautiful, beyond belief – but oh! for our dear Highland air & solitude! How different that is. And everyone of us feels it. – We have had a gt deal of rain, since that frightful heat on Saturday or Sunday when there was a stifling chirocco – der Föhn Wind – On Monday when we had settled to go to Engelberg – it poured, so we gave it up – & then cleared, – & we had a fine drive – but nothing long, in the afternoon. The drives about here however are quite beautiful & I am totally unmolested.

Yesterday we again settled to go to Engelberg & again had to give it up. We started at 10 & went as far as Stanzstadt by steamer but it rained & the mist hung so low that we gave it up – & went to Brunnen. Here we disembarked (we

'Turning up by a small village we came upon Lake Lowertz, along the banks of which we drove. In the centre is a small island & there are the ruins of an old Castle Schwanau.' (Journal, 18 August 1868)

Landslide of 1806, Goldau.
'As one passes along the Lake, one comes upon great scenes of devastation, which continue for at least a mile. Rocks & stones are hurled about in every direction, many to a distance of 100 yards, & some are of gigantic size. 1400 people are said to have perished.' (Journal, 18 August 1868)

always take our Carriages with us on board) & drove thro' Schwytz – by the lovely lake of Lowertz to Goldau where there was that most extraordinary & wonderful landslip of the Rossberg – on wh. occasion the stones were hurled to an <u>immense distance,</u> – the whole having the appearance of a mighty ruin. Here in a quiet spot overlooking the lake we lunched (Louise, Leopd., Ly. Ely, Col. Ponsonby & Mr Duckworth were with us) – a guide, Brown & Archie (who go about unmolested or noticed in their <u>Kilts</u>) attending us. Unfortunately it rained a little the whole time. We then drove thro' <u>Goldau – Arth</u> charmingly situated on the Lake of Zug at the foot of the Rigi, – (by this time it cleared & became <u>vy</u> fine & vy hot again) – we drove along the lake under trees – such beautiful Wallnut* trees, beeches etc. & vegetation I never saw – on to <u>Zug</u>, a most picturesque old Town – beautifully situated – to Cham – a sort of 1/2 way Hse., – near a Station, where we had to wait 3/4 of an hour, for our horses to rest. And we were obliged to take our tea (brought with us) in a stuffy Tea-garden, near a Skittle ground!! No one was there & not a soul knew us, but it was very <u>unpoetic</u>. Then I <u>sketched</u> & we drove home – at the rate of 3 miles an hour – by 8.[98]

* The Queen's spelling.

Reporting on the Queen's condition to Disraeli, the gentle Lady Jane Ely came out with another masterpiece of understatement: 'I think The Queen has suffered a good deal from the heat & Her Majesty finds the air a little too relaxing for her here. ... I know you will not betray me about it, but The Queen looks languid & tired I think.'[99]

Woman in local costume. Sketch by Princess Louise

In other words, she was under the weather and something had to be done about it. At this stage many a twentieth-century holidaymaker would have given up and gone home. But not Victoria Regina. She had come for bracing air and bracing air was what she was going to get. A planned expedition to the lakes of Brienz and Thun, taking in Interlaken, was abandoned and the courier Kanné despatched to reconnoitre one of the highest Alpine passes, the Furka which, as the Queen put it in her Journal, 'he thinks may be a good place for me to get some pure, fresh mountain air'.[100]

Jane Ely promised Disraeli to write and tell him 'how the change answers. ... You must not be anxious about The Queen, for I am sure it is only the heat of the weather that affects her, for Her Majesty eats and sleeps well.'[101]

Meanwhile, even during this week of frustration, there were consolations in the form of short spells of bearable, even good weather.

> *August 17*
> *A bright fine afternoon. Drove with Baby & Mary B., at the back of the town, up a high hill by Adligenschwyl, a small village, through a beautiful wood where we stopped for tea. Everywhere quantities of blackberries (of which we have excellent tarts) & heather, which made it feel quite like dear Scotland. Walked a short way & then drove by rather a steep hill, home by Seeburg & the town. The mountains glowed again in the setting sun & looked too beautiful. The town is very gay, so many people of every kind & sort out on the Parade & some very curious figures! It was pleasant, but very damp. – Janie E. read to me after dinner.*

Another source of comfort to the Queen must have been the realization that her incognita was being respected everywhere. She was not being mobbed by her own subjects or by other tourists, as Stanley had feared. The

Swiss were showing exemplary reticence and courtesy and, snug in her little pension up on the hill, she was away from prying eyes and safe from intruders – except one.

An unknown man had been stopped in the grounds of the pension trying to gain entrance and saying he needed to see the Queen. First suspicions that he was a terrorist (it would not have been the first attempt on the Queen's life) were dispelled, and when it turned out that the intruder was English he was taken under police custody to the British Legation in Berne. The rest of the story was told by the British Minister Lumley, writing to Lord Stanley:

> On the 19th inst. I received from Sir Thomas Biddulph a telegram from Lucerne to the following effect: 'There is a man named Wood who seems mad and who wants to see the Queen. The police have sent him today at half past one to the British Consul, Berne. Can you get him sent to England or away.'
>
> Yesterday evening the man was brought to the Legation by a gendarme and, as I was not in Town, he was sent to my house in the country in a hired conveyance ...
>
> The man, who was shabbily dressed, said he was an architect in search of employment. He appeared to be a harmless monomaniac, his fixed idea being that he had a secret mission to the Queen, which necessitated his immediate return to Lucerne. He complained that his effects, consisting of a small hand bag, had been searched by British detectives at Lucerne & that some important papers had been taken from him, that he had not been allowed to remain at Lucerne long enough to receive money which he expected in a day or two, and that he had been sent in charge of the police from Lucerne to Berne where he found himself without the means of paying for a night's lodging.
>
> I told him he had committed a misdemeanour in endeavouring to force his way into the Queen's residence; that as long as he was in Switzerland he would doubtless be under the surveillance of the police & that if he chose to remain in this country I could do nothing for him, but that if he made up his mind to return to England I would pay his expenses.
>
> He said that as his mission had failed he would prefer going to England; I accordingly paid his lodging for the night, had a second class place taken for him by the early train this morning for London & gave him a small sum for his food on the way.
>
> The enclosed account contains a statement of the expenses I have incurred in this business, which I shall be obliged if your Lordship will direct to be repaid to me through my Agent at the Foreign Office.[102]

The statement included SFr. 1 for a room in a pension, SFr. 1.50 for breakfast and SFr. 2.50 for dinner with wine. The incident was widely reported, with first suppositions that the man was a Fenian giving way to later rectification along the lines of Lumley's letter.

There is no mention of the incident in the Queen's Journal as we have it. Either she did not deem it worthy of mention, or Princess Beatrice omitted to copy what the Queen had written. Perhaps she was not even told of the incident on the day it happened. In any case, Kanné soon returned from his reconnaissance trip, having seen the inn on the Furka and found it good, and preparations got under way for a few days' stay there.

Yet there were still affairs of state that engaged the Queen's sense of duty and disturbed her conscience. For example, she had grave reservations about a candidate for a Church appointment whom Disraeli was urging upon her. In Switzerland the Queen could shed many of her royal burdens, but not her preoccupation with steering the Church of England down a middle course – a concern given urgency by the predominant role played by the Church in the life of her subjects. It left her only once for a few days. To ensure that her forthcoming stay in the mountains would be a real holiday within her holiday, the Queen gave instructions that no official papers were to be sent up after her. This was to be the climax of three years of hoping, scheming and planning.

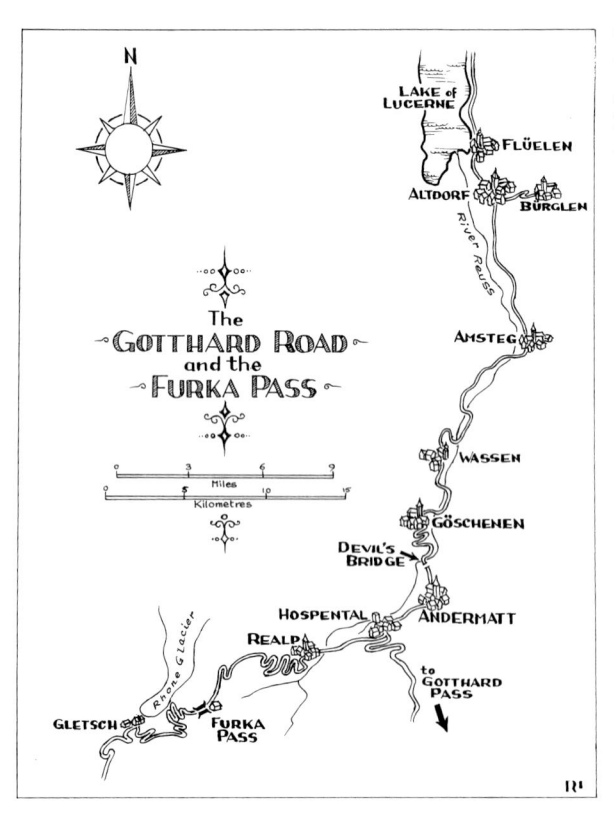

The route of Queen Victoria's most adventurous excursion in Switzerland, 22 to 25 August 1868

5 'Purer, Lighter Mountain Air'

When the Queen left Lucerne early in the morning of 22 August she had spent two weeks in or fairly near the sheltered environment of the Pension Wallis. What she was now embarking on in her quest for 'fresher, purer, lighter air' (as she put it in a letter to her daughter Victoria[103]) was a far cry indeed from her usual afternoon drives. It was nothing less than a journey into the high Alps, first up the valley leading to the St Gotthard Pass, one of Europe's great north-south routes, then (turning off before the pass itself) up to the Furka Pass, well above the tree-line, and far higher than the Queen had ever been before. She proudly noted the height in her Journal.

> *August 22*
> *Hotel Furca*
> *8,000 ft. high*
> *Got up early, & at a 1/4 p. 8 left Lucerne with Louise & Janie E., driving quickly down to the steamer, where we embarked & found Sir T. Biddulph & Sir Wm. Jenner. The mist still hung heavily on the mountain tops but gradually lifted & the Lake looked lovely as we steamed to Fluellen, which we reached in an hour. Got at once into our carriages, there being 3 besides our own, in which I went with Louise & Janie E.,*

(*below*) Flüelen, starting point of the road leading to the St Gotthard and the Furka (*below right*) Tell's chapel at Bürglen

Hoffmann on the box, & Brown behind. We went with the usual Poste very well driven with 4 small horses with bells on their harness. Sir T. Biddulph & Sir Wm. Jenner followed directly behind, & then the maids & men servants, the luggage behind, all with 4 horses & bells. Went straight up into the splendid mountains. Three miles beyond Fluellen, we came to Altorf, the capital of the canton Uri, also extremely picturesque. Passed over a bridge over the rapid stream of Schächen & saw the village of Burgh, where Tell was born & a small Chapel commemorates where his house is supposed to have stood. We soon came to where one looks up Surenen Pass, behind which Engelberg lies, immensely high mountains rise on either side. Several poor women came up to the carriage with baskets of fruit, one of which we took, gladly eating its contents, as we were very hot & thirsty. We next reached Amsteg, quite in the mountains. From there the road ascends & one goes along the rapid, foaming, dashing Reuss which forms constant waterfalls, the valley narrows, & one has the most grand mountains before one. Almost up to

Wassen

the very tops one can see those picturesque little châlets dotted about with the brightest greenest grass. I wish I could describe properly the beauty of all. Though the sun was scorching, the air was pleasant & cool in the shade. At about 1, came to Wasen, very finely situated, where we stopped outside to take our luncheon & give the horses a rest. Went on again, winding along & crossing bridges over the Reuss. Half an hour brought us to the Göschenen Thal, where the scenery became very wild, & assumed very much the character of our Highlands, only much higher and grander. A few fir trees grow amongst the rocks & even a little hay was being made and collected, where one could not imagine a goat could go.

Normal practice in a small country where, especially in Alpine valleys, every inch of arable soil is precious. Apart from the near-inaccessibility of the mountainside terrain, there was the ever-present danger of avalanches, falling rocks and landslides to contend with.

> *... August 22*
> *Got out & walked a little & again when we came to the celebrated Devil's Bridge. The road is very steep, but broad & there is plenty of room for carriages to pass one another. In spite of very sharp corners & the tremendous height at which one finds oneself overlooking yawning & frightful precipices beneath, I did not feel frightened, for the horses were extremely quiet & the driver very good.*

For centuries, travellers crossing the Alps had felt very frightened indeed. In 1188 the monk John de Bremble on his way to Rome summed up the general feeling: 'Pardon me for not writing, I have been on the Mount of Jove, on the one hand looking up to the heavens of the mountains, on the other shuddering at the hell of the valleys. Feeling myself so much nearer heaven that I was more sure that my prayer would be heard, Lord, I said, restore me to my brethren that I may tell them that they come not to this place of torment.' And a century later Adam of Usk had to be blindfolded on his way over the St. Gotthard Pass.

New and old Devil's Bridges

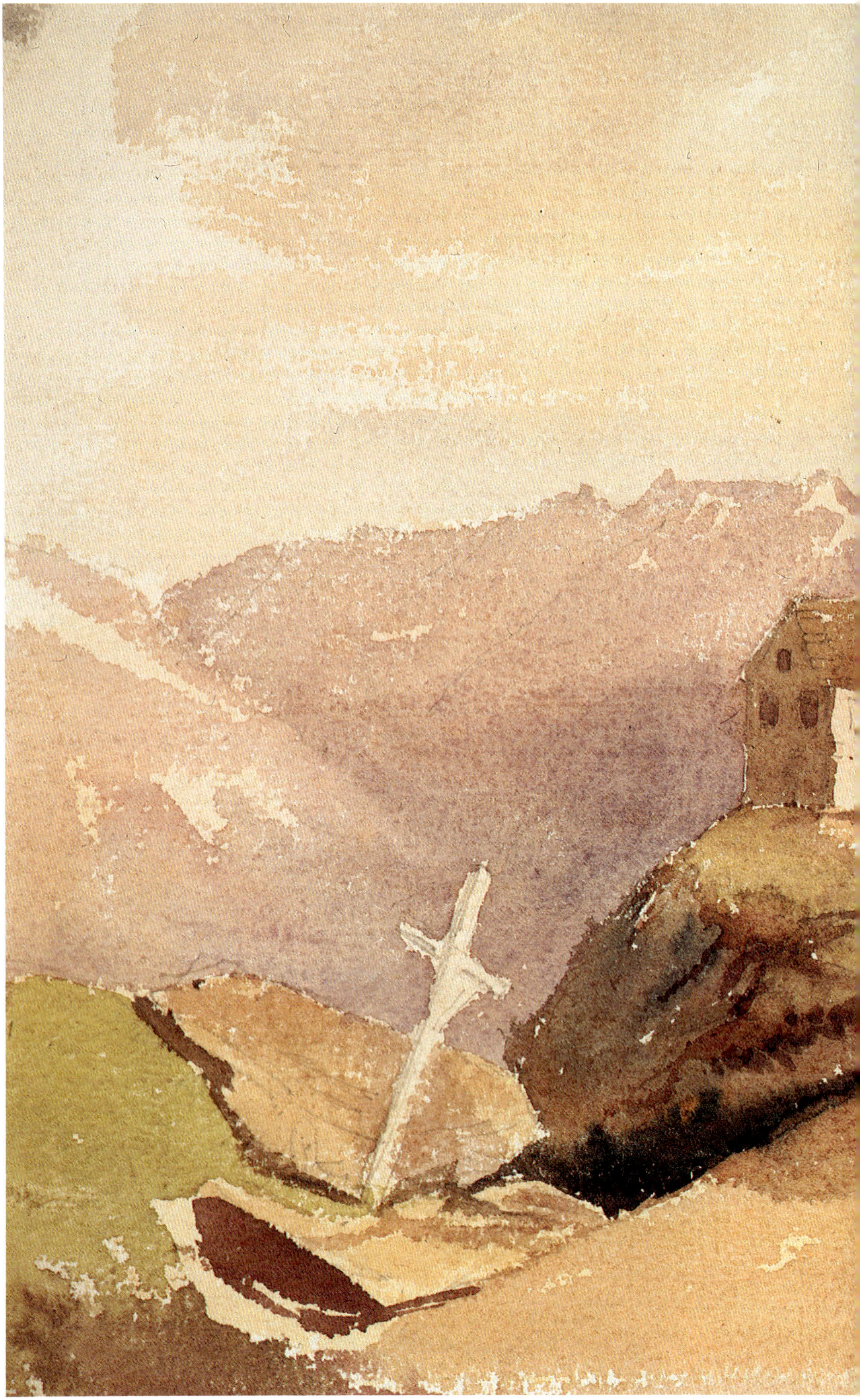

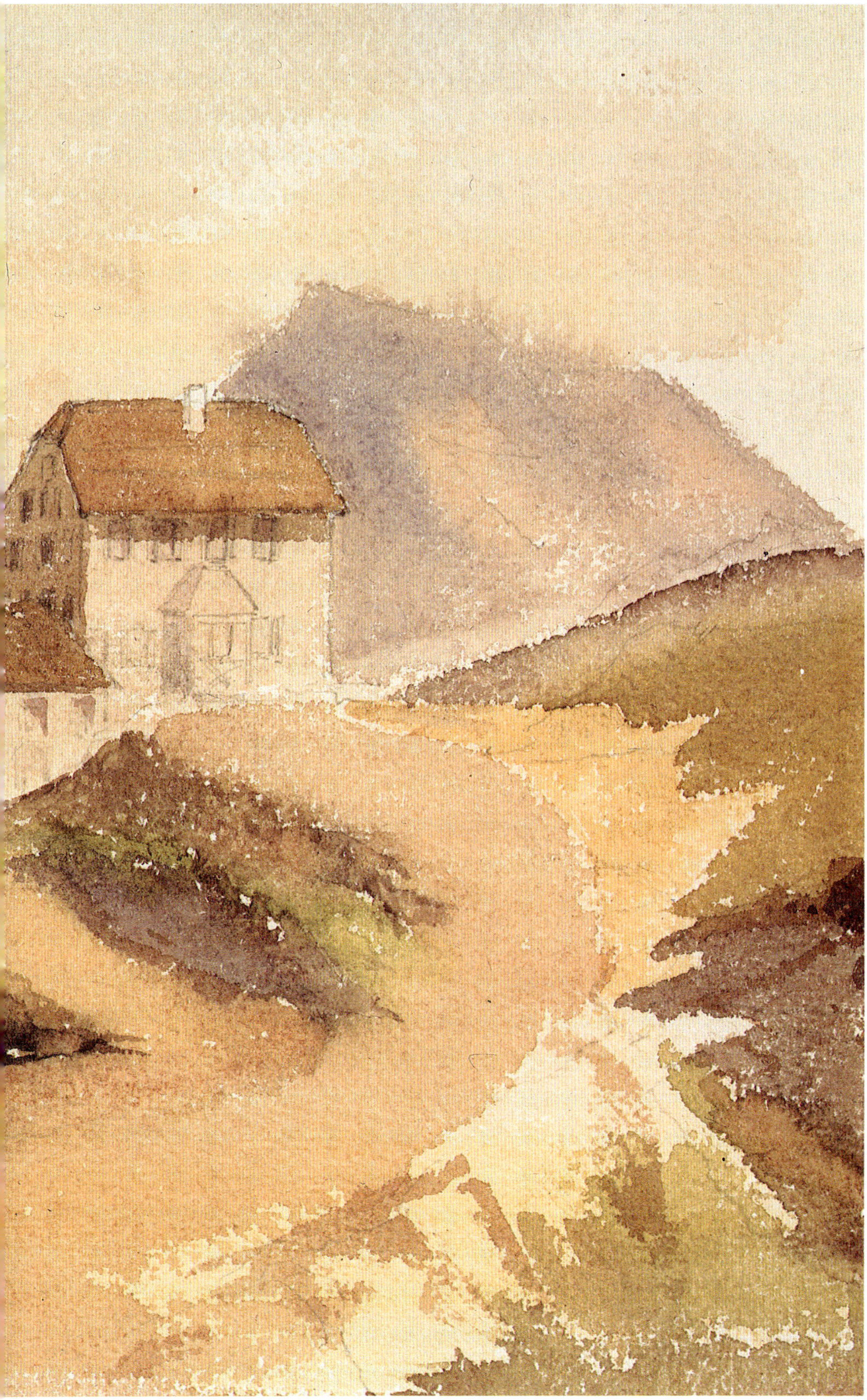

... August 22
At the Devil's Bridge the waterfall is so immense, that one feels the spray in one's face. It is magnificent, & we were all enchanted. How wonderful to think of the French Army having marched over this fearful pass & before the splendid new bridge was built. The old ruined one is still to be seen. The whole is called the St. Gothard road, but this is the Göschenen Pass. Passed through two tunnels which were built to prevent the avalanches regularly sweeping the road away. We met many tourists in carriages & on foot with 'Alpenstöcke'. In a short time we emerged from this tremendous Pass, & came upon a large flat where Andermatt lies. Further on we came to Hospenthal where the character of the houses changed, the wooden châlets there being stone ones instead. Here we changed horses, as well as our excellent driver, who had driven us with the same horses from Fluellen, about 24 miles! Instead of going up the St. Gothard we went straight on, passing Realp, another little village, where the Inn is kept by a monk whom we saw standing at the door. Very shortly after Realp, we began the tremendous ascent of the Furca, over the Sidli Alp, which took us 3 hours till we reached the desolate little Inn. As we rose we saw the Spitzenhoerner, rising up in the strangest points. The whole of this road which goes up in zig-zags has only been made since 2 years. Unfortunately the mist began to come down, & as we got higher & higher it became very cold & damp. Kanné was in a great state of fidget to hurry us on. At length, just as we came in sight of the desolate little house, the mist cleared off enough for us to see what was close to us & by 7 we reached our destination. It is in fact a miserable little 'Schenke', very small rooms poorly & badly furnished, but clean, & not uncomfortable, if there were only fireplaces as one would find in every small Highland Inn. I have a small room opening into the dining room, which I can use as a sitting room, & up a small stair case are our bedrooms. Got our dinner at 1/2p. 8. It blew dreadfully & rained, & was very cheerless.

(*previous pages*) Furka, road and inn where the Queen stayed for three nights. Watercolour by Princess Louise, 23 to 24 August 1868

Not as cheerless, though, as the welcome that had awaited a weary Swiss traveller the night before. He poured out his indignation in a letter to the Berne newspaper *Der Bund*, which (with an upsurge of republican spirit for once getting the better of its otherwise friendly attitude towards the Queen) published it under a prominent headline:

The Countess of Kent on the Furka

The following has been sent to us by a reader: It was last Friday evening towards half past seven, when, hungry and sore from a strenuous walk, I arrived at the local inn at the Furka pass, where I intended to take accommodation for the night. The dusk had already set in, thick clouds of mist were hanging in the air and it was getting uncomfortably cold. I had come from

Hasli im Hof via Grimsel and Rhonegletscher; no wonder my eyes were glowing in anticipation as I hurried towards the cosy inn. It lies about 50 paces off the side of the road, where a waiter, dressed in a black tail-coat, and a female colleague had already taken their position to welcome arriving guests (as I assumed).

Determined to evade a lengthy welcoming ceremony, I proceeded towards the house across the grass. Suddenly I heard the voice of the waiter calling from behind. 'You wish to stay at the hotel? I am sorry, but it is not open to receive guests today. The whole hotel is reserved for the Queen of England for the next three days.'

I was thunderstruck, unable to believe my own ears.

'Impossible,' I cried. 'It would be utterly foolish of the Queen to monopolize the only house on the pass for herself.'

'But it is so,' the waiter replied, 'you will have to look for other accommodation, I am afraid.'

'Well, since the Queen has taken up all the rooms, I wouldn't mind sleeping (in a rudimentary bedstead) in the hall,' I told the waiter.

'I am sorry I cannot oblige you, Sir, but I have been ordered not to let anyone into the hotel.'

'So, have the Queen and her retinue arrived yet?' I demanded to know.

'No, she is expected tomorrow or the day after tomorrow.'

'But that is preposterous,' I cried, realizing that about half a dozen irate wayfarers, among them an elderly lady, had gathered in front of the hotel, joining me in my angry protest. The grumbling and complaining which now ensued would have created quite a stir in Her Gracious Majesty's ears. Some began to circle the house in search of another entrance, but to no avail: the Queen's cook in ordinary, standing guard at the entrance, seemed quite determined to defend it with his life. – To cut a long story short, we had to leave, whether we liked it or not, if we wanted to find a place to rest our weary bones. Some of us went towards the Rhone glacier; I myself, however, decided to walk on towards Realp, where I finally arrived at 9.30 in the evening, hungry, tired out and utterly infuriated. As I was told then and several times since, many travellers were turned back in the same rude manner that day, and they all complained about the appalling impudence with which they had been treated. It seems indeed rather impudent of the Queen to book the only inn on the pass without notifying wayfarers and to have it closed to the public long before she has even arrived. The inn-keeper who lends his name to such questionable practices in my opinion deserves to be publicly denounced.

As we see it, the whole incident can be ascribed to the excessive zeal of the Queen's retinue and the avarice of the inn-keeper.

In reply to this complaint the proprietor said he had indeed turned away guests but that travellers had been notified by his colleagues earlier along the route and he had even set up a little stand in one of the outbuildings offering food for famished travellers. And anyway, he was quick to point out, the traveller in question was 'ill-natured, comported himself rudely and threatened to smash the door'.

The Queen's descent upon the hotel got around: the American J.H.B. Latrobe remarked on it in his book, *Hints for Six Months in Europe*, published in Philadelphia the following year. 'The hotel of the Furca was taken possession of by the Queen of England and her suite not long after the writer's visit in 1868, and the common wayfarers were referred to a very modest shanty – it would be called in America – across the road'.

On the day the Queen travelled to the Furka, Stanley in his Lucerne hotel had raised a lordly eyebrow and written to Disraeli about 'the lady', as he was wont to refer to the Queen: 'I have only seen her once, for about ten minutes, and now she is gone to the Furca, where having taken the whole of the only inn, she has practically closed the pass against travellers for three days.'[104]

WATERSHED

After her first night in the high Alps on the Furka Pass, the Queen may have been wondering whether she had made a ghastly mistake in letting herself be brought all this way only to freeze in bed and be blanketed in fog. She even complained about the cold – and for her, that meant something. On the other hand, she may have been restless because she was not yet acclimatized to the rarified air at that altitude.

Very likely the Queen did not lose sleep through feeling guilty, or being sorry for the travellers whom her courier Kanné had edged out of the inn she was occupying. In fact, she had probably not even been told. Such sordid details may well have been kept from her: her stay on the Furka was going to be the zenith of her whole holiday in Switzerland and she would need to be shielded from anything as unpleasant as this. There was something else to keep her awake.

> *August 23*
> *Woke frequently from the cold. There were only 42 degrees in my room! There was a dense fog & occasional snow & sleet. The people were not hopeful of its improving. – After our breakfast remained writing till 11, when I said I really* must *go out. Suddenly at that moment, the sun came out, allowing the splendid mountain tops, rearing their heads to the very clouds to be seen. Some were tipped & some entirely covered with snow.*

This was the turning point of the Queen's stay in Switzerland. As the sun broke through that morning, her holiday finally fell into place.

> *... August 23*
> *Walked with Louise & Janie E., Hoffmann & Brown following on the road leading to the Rhone Glacier & on to Brinz, about a mile. We were*

in the greatest admiration of the splendid panorama before us, all the mountains so softly lit up, white with snow & with the loveliest blue tints. The Weisshorn & Randenhorn, the former, one of the highest peaks in Switzerland, were pointed out to us, also the Fleschhorn & Wasserhorn, which are close to the Simplon. We could see the Todtensee, a small lake, quite high up, where a number of French were thrown in, which gave that dreadful name to the lake. Close to the Hotel are the Matterhorn* & another smaller, very dirty looking glacier. One is quite in the midst of them! The air is most beautiful & light, & enabled me to accomplish, what was quite a long walk for me. We met many carriages, all of a primitive kind & tourists on foot with their napsacks & Alpenstöcke. Heard the curious whistle of the marmottes. – When I came in read Prayers, etc. Lunched below as we dined. Both gentlemen greatly delighted by the scenery & air. – Afterwards started with Louise & Janie E. in the sociable, with only a pair of horses, for the glacier, driving along part of the road we had walked in the morning, & on a mile & 1/4 we came to the 1st corner of this most wonderful and precipitous road & in another moment came, as it were, quite close upon the glacier, the effect of which cannot be described. One can hardly believe it is real, it seems almost like something unearthly! The road descends in 7 great zig-zags & with this marvellous glacier piled up in huge boulders of solid ice, with peaks like rocks, looked so alarming & steep, that I asked to walk down. It was really more alarming to <u>look at</u> than <u>in reality</u> to drive. We went down quite slowly & then trotted along the road which overlooks the

Upper part of Rhone Glacier. Watercolour by Queen Victoria, 23 to 24 August 1868

* One of the Queen's very few topographical errors or perhaps a mistake made by Princess Beatrice in her transcription. What she saw was the Muttenhorn (sometimes spelt Muthorn), to the south of the Furka. The Matterhorn is far away and well out of view from around the Furka.

glacier, the level mass of which looks as if it had come down like soup & hardened.

… August 23
After 1/2 a mile we stopped and got out, intending to go down on to the glacier. They wanted to carry me in a chaise à porteur, down the steep bank above it, but I refused & with the help of an Alpenstock & Brown's strong arm got down all right. When we came to the roughest highest bank of stones I would not go any further but let Louise go on with Hoffmann & Brown, to the glacier, sitting down & watching them with Janie E., talking to the good humoured Swiss men in their blue blouses, who had wanted to carry me. Louise & her companions went on a good long way, stepping across some of the crevasses. When they came back, I was carried up & we got into the carriage again, & took our tea. A large herd of at least 100 cattle were grazing on the hillside, with nice bells round their necks. Went on a little after our tea & sketched as we went up very slowly, gazing with astonishment at the marvellous glaciers. Home by 1/4 to 7. The air, brisk & cold.

View from the Queen's sitting room in the inn on the Furka, by Princess Louise, 24 August 1868

August 24

There had been a frost in the night, but the day was perfectly splendid, & the mountains so clear. After breakfast remained sketching the splendid view from one of the windows. At 11 walked out with Janie E., going first upon a very small glacier below the house, where I picked up some fine crystals & found some pretty flowers. Lovely blue gentians were brought down from the Gothenstock for me. There seem to be so many flowers that are not seen elsewhere. Then walked with both Louise & Janie, the same way as yesterday. The sun was so warm & the view so splendidly clear. Got a little way up the hillside, at the foot of the Furcahorn, & sat down & sketched. On our way out we looked at the cows, small, but so pretty, which had come much nearer & talked to the boy who was herding them. He showed us the curious stick with 2 leather thongs attached to a chain, fastened to it, which he uses to drive the cows with. – Resting & writing – out driving at 1/2p.3 on, & down the same fearful road as yesterday. Twice we had to meet carriages & were going down on the outside which terrified me, though I was astonished at not minding it more. We again gazed with wonder & astonishment at the splendid glacier. When we got down, we found 2 horses quietly waiting, which the coachman (a careful good driver) fastened on behind our carriage & thus we trotted on, quite to the foot of the glacier, where the Rhone runs out from underneath it, in a thick white stream. Went up to the Hotel du Rhone Glacier, where a good many people seemed to be stopping. Here, we had to get out, however we got on as quickly as we could, & Alpenstock in hand, walked about 1/2 a mile along a path, crossing a little stream over rough stones, till we came to the glacier itself where it was level. With the help of Brown & Hoffmann I walked a little way on it & back. It cracked a little, but the thickness of the ice is quite enormous. It looks brown & rather dirty.

The same view from the Queen's sitting room. Watercolour by Queen Victoria, 24 August 1868

Louise then went to a cavern with Sir T. Biddulph, which is scooped out in the ice a good long way. I walked slowly back to where Hoffmann had kindled a fire, & where we sat on the grass under a small bank, watching the water boil in a <u>casserole</u>, a <u>kettle</u> being unknown in these parts. Had some delicious tea, then hurried off to our carriage, to which 4 horses were now attached. Went off in grand style, the whip being well smacked & the good little horses encouraged by that peculiar 'hau-ip', which the men here constantly call to them. On the level we got on fast, then came that tremendous long ascent of certainly 1000 ft., which took us 5 quarters of an hour to accomplish. We met men, who go up daily into the mountains to milk the cows, & carry milk & butter, even cheese, on their backs. Often these are conveyed in small carts, drawn by poor dogs.

From the foot of Furkahorn. Watercolour by Queen Victoria, 24 August 1868

> *The moon shone out over the glacier, as we were driving back & it & the mountains looked too beautiful. Hoffmann & the driver yodelled as we went along. Got in at 1/2p. 7.*

Next morning the time had come for Queen Victoria, now tingling with mountain air, to return to her pension in Lucerne.

> *August 25*
> *The morning was rather dull & misty. – Slept extremely well & did not suffer from the cold, though there had been snow in the night. Never had a better appetite, the air reminded me so much of that in our dear Highlands. – At 1/2p. 10 we left the Furca, where ... we had spent a most interesting time, & I shall ever look back with pleasure & thankfulness, to have been able to see all these wonderful works of nature. Everyone, high & low, was so amiable, cheerful & helpful & we lived so completely together like a family, that the recollection of it will be most pleasant. The luggage started before us, but the 3 other carriages kept together with ours. Came down very quickly & that very steep part seemed as nothing to us, in comparison with the 1st day. The Febia (sic) was well seen, as we left the little house standing in all its wild solitude. We walked down part of the steepest part, as I wished to warm my feet. Came down in an hour & 40 m. to Hospenthal, having taken 3 hours to go up! Here we changed horses, getting our excellent driver of the preceding day, who Hoffmann says is the best in the country! We came very shortly in sight of the Devil's Bridge, where we got out to look at the waterfall & admire the stupendous rocks, which are so grand & wild. Walked a little way & met a whole party of Pifferari, in their most picturesque, though dirty dress, who were returning to their native place Caserta. They began to play their bagpipes (3 men, with about 4 or 5 boys). There was a little imp who kept dancing about, more like a monkey than anything else, holding his*

On the St Gotthard road after Wassen ('*Wasen*') Sketch by Queen Victoria, 25 August 1868

black Calabrian hat for money. The next rencontre was a string of 5 diligences, who were toiling up the very steep ascent. Got into the carriage again, driving as far as the Göschenen Bridge, where we scrambled up to some level grass, above the road & sat down to have our luncheon. Remained sketching for a while, then drove past Göschenen & looked up the splendid Pass of Süsten, which goes up to a glacier of the same name, – past the Teufel's Stein, an immense stone just above the river. Stopped shortly after Wasen, to make a sketch as the scenery from there had a totally different character, but we were pressed for time. Went on very quickly through beautiful country, passing the Pfaffensprung, where a Priest is supposed to have jumped with a young girl across the river! At Amsteg we watered our horses & took 2 leaders, then drove slowly on to Altdorff & Fluellen, which we reached at 1/2p. 5, going at once on board the steamer, where our luggage had already been for 2 hours. Off we steamed, & had one very heavy shower of rain & a great deal of wind. We were glad to get our tea on board. Got home at 1/4 to 8 & found dear Arthur & Col. Elphinstone, who are staying at Lucerne & arrived 2 days ago.* We talked much at dinner of all we had seen. –

While the Queen was away on this expedition with Princess Louise, Lady Ely, Sir Thomas Biddulph and the solicitous Sir William Jenner, those who stayed behind (the other two children, Leopold and Beatrice, Lady Biddulph, Colonel Ponsonby, the Revd. Duckworth and Miss Bauer) were left to their own devices at Lucerne. Ponsonby caught the spirit of how they spent their time in a letter to his wife:

Upon the 'Cats away the Mice will play' principle, we are going it. We went out this morning at 9 and tomorrow at 8.30 so I haven't time to write much as we are out all day. Today we went to Alpnacht & then drove to Lungern, had luncheon in a field & rambled in woods. Leopold and Beatrice quite delighted – Mary Bids low at seeing beautiful distant alps and not being at Furka – and so home. On my way I met Ld Stanley's private Secretary who with Ld S are furious with me ... They got a telegram from England that all were anxious about the Q. and the Fenians and he Ld S knows nothing. Yet it turns out there has been an arrest and he Ld S was never informed of it. I tried to pacify him. There was an arrest I know but of a mere idiot. He wrote to ask to see the Q and Baker the policeman being sent to him found he was half foolish – & communicated with the Swiss police and he was sent home to his friends. It

---

* Prince Arthur, the Queen's third son was on a tour of Switzerland with his Governor, staying at a Lucerne hotel because there was no room at the pension.

may have been wrong of Bids not to tell Ld S but really it was so trifling an affair he thought nothing of it. Of course till he returns I cannot say – but I think in my own mind he ought to have told Ld S. So they have written me a little letter which I am to give Bids. However all that nonsense abt Fenians is bosh ... Much talk of the danger of the St. Gotthard road – which she had been led to expect – but didn't find. The latter part beautiful – so like the Spittal of Glenshee!! The Furka itself like Lough ... [illegible] ... (St Paul's like Crathie Church just as much) the air clear and Scotch etc. To Helena a full description of the road up 'I can scarcely believe it is Sunday' says D ... Mr Woodruffe the clergyman here has gone up the Rigi but hinted he had gone to officiate at the Furka – which is generally believed here. – D indignant at the appt of Hugh McNeile to be Dean of Ripon a regular electioneering apptmt – and is so afraid that Peterboro will also be the same. Bids writes from Furka that it is fine – but very cold – only stoves there and very small but comfortable. They had all been to see the Rhone Glacier.[105]

Sunrise, 4 a.m. as seen from Pension Wallis, Lucerne, 1868. Watercolour by Princess Louise

6 Exploration

Having tasted true Alpine air, Queen Victoria now wanted more, and Central Switzerland certainly had much more to offer – not only air but spectacular views and a variety of places to explore.

The next stage of the Queen's Swiss stay consisted of a number of active – some even ambitious – one-day excursions during which she could top up on bracing mountain air as well as experience and glory in new sights and places. Each of these expeditions alternated with a day of rest.

To begin with, she spent a quiet day in and around the pension, resting after her long return journey from the Furka. It happened to be the departed Prince Albert's birthday, which the Queen invariably commemorated:

> *August 26*
> *This dear blessed day came round again! How changed now, but I always try to keep it as a holiday, & make it bright & cheerful. I know my beloved one would wish me to be cheerful, & would rejoice in seeing me take an interest in all I see. Gave all the Children trifles. Arthur came up to breakfast, which we had out of doors. Dawdled about a little & wrote some letters in the summer house. – Drove in the afternoon with the 4 Children, as I always like to do on this beloved day, going in 2 carriages. Took our tea with us. A very fine evening. Coming back we dropped Arthur near the Schweizer Hof.*

Strengthened after this day of rest, the Queen was now looking forward to going up the Rigi – by then the best known mountain far and wide, and one she saw every time she looked across the lake from the pension. Foremost in her mind will have been the thought that it was from the Rigi that Prince Albert in 1837 had sent her the cherished alpine rose which she took with her wherever she went.

> *August 27*
> *At 10 started … & went on board the steamer on which we took our ponies & grooms. In about 40 minutes we reached Weggis, quite a small quiet place, where the ponies were at once disembarked & 2 horses of the country were provided for Janie E. & Col. Ponsonby, Arthur insisting on*

walking. Mounted our ponies, 4 Swiss men leading the other horses & carrying the luncheon & tea baskets, cloaks, etc. There was a good deal of mist in the mountains, but the sun was very hot. Directly behind the small town, the ascent began & at once dreadfully steep. We had gone but a short way when all on foot took off their coats. We met many funny looking people coming down, mules carrying their luggage piled up on their packs, and we saw ladies being carried in chaises à porteur. Hoffman called out frequently to us to stop & rest a little. The road winds along in constant sight of the Lake, but it was very misty & we had no good view. When we came to a spring, the poor sweating horses & streaming men, had a drink. For a short while there was some very steep climbing. At length we came in sight of Rigi Kalt Bad, about 1200 ft. below the summit, which is 5,910 ft. & as everyone seemed overpowered

Inn on the way up the Rigi

with the heat, we stopped about 10 minutes in the shade afforded by another small châlet, where refreshments were sold. In a few more minutes we got to the Rigi Kalt Bad, an immense Hotel, where people stay. 2 or 300 people turned out, & as we passed under the Hotel, a Band struck up 'God save the Queen' & people fired off some little guns, at a distance ... Halted once more & then went up in another 1/2 hour to the Rigi Rothstock just below & opposite the Rigi Staffel, another Hotel in sight of the Rigi Kulm. Reached this at 1/2 p. 1, & in a shady place sat down on the grass to rest & have our well earned luncheon. It had cleared very much & the splendid Alps of the Bernese Oberland were seen to great advantage. There are quantities of beautiful blue gentians growing on the top, & all the way up & down. We remained here about 3/4 of an hour & looked down on Rigi Klosterli. Mounted our ponies again & rode in another 1/2 hour to the Rigi Kulm, where there is a very large Hotel where people stay the night, in order to see the sun rise. We

On the way from Kaltbad to Rigi Staffel and Rigi Kulm

did not get off, but remained at the top for about 10 minutes gazing at the splendid view. We saw, though not very clearly, an immense way all over the flat land & the Lakes of Lucerne, Zug, etc. on the one side & on the other, all the finest, highest mountains of the Bernese Alps, with their snowy peaks. There were 3 stalls with things to buy & a high sort of stand, people climbed up to see the view.... Rode a little over the other side looking down on Goldau, the Lake of Lowerz & the Muota Thal. Then we left. I got off & walked nearly as far as the Staffel, then mounted my pony again, & came down an easier way, reaching Untersee baden, (a fort at the foot of the steep part of the Rigi), at about 5. There, in a meadow, we had our tea, getting some hot water from a little inn. Remained nearly 3/4 of an hour & sketched a little, then went on, a steep descent winding through lanes overhung with endless fruit trees, getting in another 3/4 of an hour to Küsnacht, where at the end of the town we found our carriages & drove home as quickly as we could by Seeberg, dropping Arthur near the Schweizer Hof. Got back at 8, all feeling, that it had been a most successful day. – Only 4 to dinner. –

That night the Queen slept well but noted next morning that she was very stiff. She went for a walk, wrote letters, painted, took a drive with Princess Louise, had tea in the open (recorded as usual in the Journal) and sketched *'one of the pretty Swiss houses close to Kriens'*. After dinner, Jane Ely read to her – one of the normal duties of a lady-in-waiting.

The Queen was now ready for another attempt the following day to go to Engelberg, a mountain village which was already a popular resort for British visitors. Here she was to make history by being the first female monarch –

Seeboden, on the way down from the Rigi. Watercolour by Queen Victoria, 27 August 1868 (*see previous page*)

The celebrated panorama from the summit of the Rigi

and even more remarkable, the first woman – to set foot in the inner sanctum of the celebrated Roman Catholic monastery of Engelberg.

The way there took the Queen and her party over the lake to Stansstad, where they disembarked and drove first to Stans.

It was two o'clock by the time they reached Engelberg.

August 29
Lunched on a grassy bank, about 10 minutes distance from the village. We sketched a little afterwards, though there was no distant view & then walked to the village, to see the Monastery, which is a curious one, from its great antiquity. We first stopped at a Châlet, close to the road, where a nice looking but very poor girl was weaving silk. There were hardly any people in the village, but 2 or 3 had their suspicion, as to who we were. We walked by the Gasthaus straight into the Church, hearing the sounds of the organ. Vespers were going on, & I went close up to the altar steps. Service was going on behind the rails, reminding one much of our Cathedral services. The music was very fine. We had to wait about 10 minutes until the service was over, as we wanted to go over the Monastery. At the conclusion, the Priest in his golden vestments stood with the acolytes, swinging their censors before the immense High Altar. Then all the monks, one after the other, came out & knelt in a side Chapel, where there was a most ugly image of the Madonna & Child, in a silver & gold dress. The Church is a fine large one, but white washed, & in bad taste. Directly the service was concluded Hoffmann beckoned to me to come on & we went past the altar into a passage, where we were met by 2 or 3 Priests, one of whom, a younger man, showed us very civilly everything. There are 30 monks, but their dress is more like that of ordinary Priests, merely a cowl in addition to the black soutane. We were taken into the Sacristy, where we were shown their fine Plate & very rich vestments, a curious old Pastoral Staff & Crucifix, likewise some vestments worn by the 1st Abbot in the 11th Century when the Monastery (for Benedictines) was founded. Some of the vestments were

'Stanz is a picturesque old town, with several Churches & a fine new monument, a marble group of Arnold Winkelried being killed & lying on the ground, with the spears in his arms.' (Journal, 29 August 1868)

'There is also an ugly old statue of him.' (Journal, 29 August 1868)
Arnold von Winkelried was a Swiss hero who helped his countrymen to victory against the Habsburgs in 1386 by stepping forward and concentrating the enemy spears upon himself, thereby opening a way into their ranks

Near Engelberg.
Sketch by Queen Victoria, 29 August 1868

marked by Agnes, wife of the Emperor Albert. A heavy smell of incense pervaded the Sacristy & lower passages. We next went up a flight of stone steps to the Library, very rich in Missals, some of which were shown us. We all wrote our names in the visitors' book, I signing myself as Countess of

Engelberg Monastery visitors' book, 29 August 1868

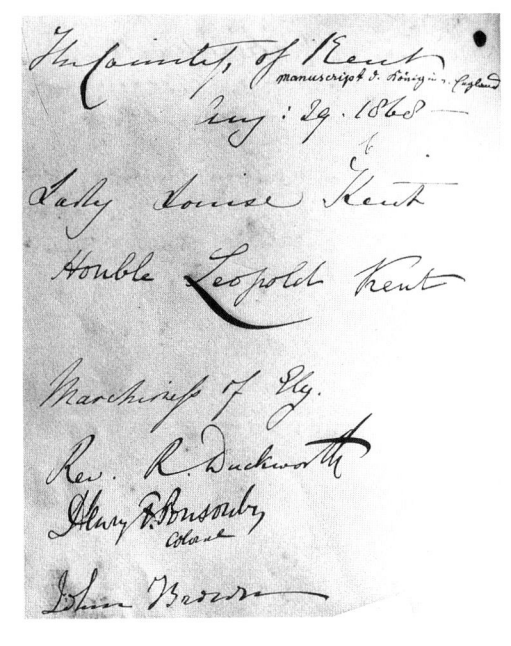

Kent & Louise & Leopold as the Lady Louise & Honble. Leopold Kent. Saw the Gallery into which open all the cells & were taken into the Principal's room, most comfortable, with a piano & violin in it, & to the large room used for ceremonies, where more embroideries were shown us. We looked into the 'Klostergarten', & then left, entering our carriages at the outer gate.

It was no mean thing for a woman to have been invited into the heart of a Roman Catholic Monastery – and the Head of the Church of England at that. The Abbot, Anselm Villiger, recorded the visit in his diary:

She came during Vespers, visited the Sacristy, the Library, the Great Hall and also desired to see a cell. She enquired about the number of monks, their way of living and daily routine etc. She was very gracious and friendly. Her retinue included a Prince, a Princess, Lord Chamberlain, Ladies-in-Waiting etc. During her excursion to Engelberg she visited only the Monastery, to the surprise of many visitors. Her bearing was very simple. It appears she had taken her midday meal in the shade of the stone on the Rüttimatt. Both she and her retinue spoke very good German. I accompanied her to the Monastery gate where a large number of visitors had gathered.

Both the Abbot and the local newspaper reported that the Queen was simply attired and not wearing a crinoline.

> *... August 29*
> *We bought some trifles & some Edelweiss, which is found near there. The horses held up badly driving down the long hill, & Benz, the coachman was nervous, having not put on properly 2 shoes, besides the break, the result being that the carriage kept twirling about, 1st one way, then the other, which frightened me very much. Instead of going to Stanzstadt we went to another picturesque village where we re-embarked & had our tea on board the steamer. It was cold & windy on the water. Got home a little before 8. –*

A quiet Sunday followed, with the Reverend Duckworth holding a service in the pension as before. The Queen turned to family matters and pondered a letter she had received from Crown Princess Victoria about her grandson, young Prince Wilhelm, the Crown Princess's son who later became Emperor of Germany from 1888 to the end of World War I. In answer the Queen wrote:

> What you told me of dear Willy interested me very much. I share your anxiety especially as regards pride and selfishness. In our days – when a Prince can only maintain his position by his character – pride is most dangerous. And then besides I do feel so strongly that we are before God all alike, and that in the twinkling of an eye, the highest may find themselves at the feet of the poorest and lowest. I have seen the noblest, most refined, high-bred feelings in the humblest and most unlearned, and this it is most necessary a Prince should feel. I am sure you, darling, who never had any pride will feel and understand this well.[106]

An afternoon drive with Louise and Arthur (with *'tea in the carriage'*[107]) gave them a fine view of Pilatus. The weather was promising well and it was decided to go up Pilatus the next day.

> *August 31*
> *A fine clear morning. – Arthur came to breakfast & at 1/2 p. 9 we drove off in 2 carriages, I with Louise & Janie E., in the sociable, Arthur & Col. Ponsonby in the next. The ponies had been sent by steamer to Alpnacht, which we drove to. The day was very pleasant & clear, but not particularly hot. The views were beautiful. Just short of the town of Alpnacht we found our ponies with 2 jaded beasts for Janie E. & Col. Ponsonby & boys to carry our luncheon &c. Started at once, Arthur walking the whole time. I rode good old 'Flora' & Louise 'Sultan'. The road, mostly dreadfully stony, loose slippery, sharp stones, very trying for both man & beast, but with the exception of the last 1/2 hour to the top,*

· *Exploration* ·

Queen Victoria and suite ascending Pilatus. (Oil painting by J.J. Zelger, 1868, commissioned by Queen Victoria)

not near so steep, though more tedious than the Rigi. We went steadily & slowly through beautiful woods of beech, spruce & silver fir. Châlets are sprinkled about here & there & many cows grazing with bells around their necks, which sounds so pretty. What makes the ascent less trying, is that one constantly comes to level parts, for a short distance. Stopped for a few minutes at a small 1/2 way house to get a little water. Soon after came to one of the prettiest spots possible, wild rocks tumbled about, with some grass & small 'Senn Hütten'. Many wild flowers grow there. In the woods there were quantities of cranberries & blaeberries & c. The views became more & more magnificent, as we emerged from the wooded parts. The sun having come out it was very hot, & feeling tired, besides being hungry, it was nearly 2, refused to go to the top, till we had had our luncheon. Sketched a little afterwards, & then remounted our ponies, riding up the very steep ascent, which was disagreeable, owing to the dreadful loose stones. In 25 minutes, however, we got to the top, where the view is most extensive & magnificent, & the air was fine & pure. We could see the following Glaciers: Blümli Alp, Ischingli, Jungfrau, Silberhorn, Moench, & Eiger, besides all the other well known nearer mountains, & the Lakes of Sarnen, Lucerne, Baldegg, Sempach &

Mauen. Our own fine Lake was beautifully seen, looking towards Fluellen. There was still one steep extreme point, called the Esel, which can only be got up to on foot, so I preferred remaining below sitting in front of the big Hotel. All, but Janie E. & Hoffmann went up & I employed my time in sketching, making some little purchases, & writing my name in the visitor's book. We had not met a soul going up, excepting 2 or 3 Senner, & the Hotel seemed quite empty. Soon after 4 we commenced our descent, I walked, not without difficulty, held by Brown's strong arm & with a good stick. Got on my pony again, where we had lunched, but the others walked on further. Passed by a spot where a cross is made on a stone & a stick placed, showing where a poor Scotch gentleman, Thomson, by name, died quite suddenly, about a week after we arrived at Lucerne, leaving a young widow at the Hotel! Rode right down to the bottom, 'Flora' going in the most perfect manner, without once making a false step. Louise walked down the greater part of the way. Stopped for about 20 minutes, to take tea, which was very welcome. We then restarted, & by this time the views became more & more glorious, the setting sun making the sky crimson & orange, while it cast that wonderful soft rosy light on the snowy peaks. Add to this the cobalt blue of the nearer wooded mountains, & the whole makes a*

Queen Victoria on *Flora* (with John Brown)

picture of indescribable beauty. The moon rose splendidly & cast a fresh beauty on everything, as the light faded away. It was getting rapidly dark as we came down, which we did by 1/2p. 7. In a moment were off in our carriages & Benz drove fast, nevertheless it was 9 before we got back, much pleased at our successful day, which not having been so hot, was less tiring than when we went up the Rigi. The drive home by moonlight, reflected in the Lake was most lovely & romantic. – We had our dinner as quickly as possible. –

By way of contrast, Lord Stanley with his Private Secretary Sanderson had 'done' Pilatus two weeks earlier, in a manner more typical of British travellers in those days. Here is his account:

Up at 5, light early breakfast. Started at 6, reached Hergeswyl in 40 minutes: engaged a man and horse in case of accidents, and began the ascent. Sanderson after walking a little way was seized with palpitations of the heart, and rode all the rest. I walked, and was glad to find that two years of sedentary life had left me still able to face a steep hill without discomfort. The first two hours of the way we were among pastures and fir-woods, with fresh running streams, and when we turned, noble views of the lakes. The last hour was passed in mounting a steep ravine covered with loose stones, by a corkscrew path, rather trying to wind and legs. Reached Klimserhorn hotel at 10 exactly, having been 3 hours on the way. Breakfast there, mounted the little hill behind the inn, lounged, then on to the highest point, 40 minutes further, through a curious cleft in the rock, where a ladder has been fixed. The height is 7300 feet, or nearly 6000 above the lake. Noble view of Bernese Alps. Back to our hotel, rambled slowly down, Hergeswyl at 5 P.M. and home by 6, well pleased with our day, and very little tired. We had not above 7 hours of walking, but on rough ground. The heat was not great on or near the top, but on coming down again we felt it oppressive.

The ascent to the Klimserhorn is about 5400 ft. from the plain, which being done in 3 hours gives 1800 ft. per hour, or 30 ft. per minute, or 6 inches per second: a rather rapid rise. Taking the weight of a full-grown man at 180 lbs., the power used is that required to lift 90 lbs. 1 foot per second: a convenient formula. In general I have found that 1200 ft. vertical rise per hour is fair work, allowing for irregularities of ground.[108]

Fair work indeed, compared to twentieth-century holiday habits. Apart from being a classical scholar, Stanley also had a degree in mathematics.

The Queen, after her own day on Mt Pilatus at the end of August, was now clearly feeling the full benefit of her holiday. There was another week to go – another week of living in the close family environment which was so precious to her. The only outside pressure was coming from the Swiss guide Hofmann with his welcome suggestions of new places to discover, new views to enjoy, and she was far away from the public responsibilities that had been so intolerably burdensome. The weather was now more settled and she complained far less about the heat. There was a new culprit: dust, which the drier air sent swirling up from roads and paths, but she took this in her stride. And it was a matter of pride to her that she was getting fitter, as she noted in her Journal the day after the great Pilatus ascent.

> *September 1*
> *A very fine, very hot morning. – Breakfast out & then writing in the summer house. – Not very tired or stiff, less so than after the expedition to the Rigi. – Saw Ld. Stanley, who spoke of poor Ld. Howard de Walden's death, quite sudden, from apoplexy.*

Howard de Walden had been British Ambassador in Belgium, a country already then caught up in the power-game between France and Prussia. In addition, the King of the Belgians was Queen Victoria's cousin. So the choice of a successor to this important post would have been of immediate concern to the Queen and her Foreign Secretary. The Queen and Lord Stanley also spoke about two other matters on this occasion. Neither are mentioned in the Queen's Journal (as transcribed by Princess Beatrice before burning the original) and both were no doubt unwelcome intrusions on her holiday – especially the first, which concerned what amounted to a game of hide and seek.

This was nothing less than another chapter in the long-running drama of the Queen's Paris Gaffe. Ever since the Queen refused to return the Empress Eugénie's call on her in Paris, and particularly as the time of her return to England via Paris approached, the British Ambassador in Paris, Lord Lyons – anxious to avoid another diplomatic disaster – had been working hard to bring about a meeting between the Empress and a reluctant Queen en route back home.

All available forces were put into action. Letters passed back and forth between Paris, Lucerne and London: Lyons to Stanley, Stanley to Disraeli, Disraeli to the Queen, Biddulph to Stanley and Lyons, Stanley to Ely, Ely to Disraeli ... Machiavellian skills were deployed on all sides, culminating in a pincer movement on the Queen. This was executed by Jane Ely and allies just before the Queen's ascent of Mount Pilatus. Flushed with victory, she hastened to tell Disraeli:

> I spoke to The Queen last evening, in consequence of Lord Stanley's anxiety about Paris & told her the soreness felt about the Empress's visit not having been returned & that it was much wished it should be paid on the return ... & that Ld Stanley mentions it through me, not wishing to do it officially. The Queen objected very much at first, but Princess Louise & Lady Biddulph backed me up & she was so nice about it, The Queen & said, she would go and see the Empress, but with as little state as possible ... Lord Stanley no doubt will tell you, but I thought I would send you this pleasant news, quietly. I hope nothing will prevent it now, it seems it is the German relations which have been the stumbling block & the feeling that they say, the Queen is more friendly to France, than Prussia, however all that will come right, forgive my indiscretion.[109]

It was Lord Stanley who delivered the coup de grâce during his interview with the Queen in her pension on 1 September, as recorded in his diary:

> Drove to Pension Wallis, saw the Queen (she kept me waiting nearly 2 hours), who had been up Pilatus yesterday on her pony. She was in good spirits and good temper: and consented to call on the Empress when passing through Paris: which is good as it stops the mouths of mischief-makers. Probably she feels that after passing the whole day in exercise she cannot well plead illness as an excuse for not doing the usual civilities. Ly Ely helped usefully to bring her to understand this, and Ld Lyons was anxious about it.[110]

The Queen had given in, but a small hope was left to her. Stanley immediately telegraphed to Lord Lyons, transmitting that hope: 'The Queen will call on the Empress if the Empress is in Paris when she passes through. But she hopes that neither the Emperor nor the Empress will alter on her account any arrangements they may have made.'[111] Aware that they had won the battle but perhaps not the war, Stanley also wrote to Disraeli: 'Dear D., I have settled with H.M. about her return. She will visit the Empress, if the latter is in Paris when she passes through. So that is all satisfactorily arranged. Even if no meeting takes place, the offer of one is something.'[112]

So far so good, but the dénouement was yet to come.

The other subject discussed between the Queen and Lord Stanley that day was the appointment of a new Bishop – a matter of constitutional importance to the Queen as Head of the Church of England, and of political importance to Disraeli as leader of the Conservative Party marshalling its forces for the forthcoming general election.

Now, on her hill above Lucerne in Switzerland, Queen Victoria, Supreme Governor of the Church of England, looked the politician Lord Stanley in the eye and spoke like the mid-nineteenth century sovereign that she was. Stanley's diary records the scene:'She talked no politics, except that speaking of the new bishop who has to be made, she said she would have neither a ritualist, nor a strong party man of any sort, but one of moderate opinions.'[113]

Writing to Disraeli, Stanley amplified on this:

> The great lady was in high spirits and good humour, and talked more freely than I had ever heard her: but not a word about politics, except about the new

Rigi. Watercolour by Queen Victoria, 3 September 1868

bishop that will have to be appointed. On that subject she said that she did not like strong partisans, they were apt to give trouble, she would have no one who leant to the ritualistic side, but should prefer a moderate man who would not give offence. I expressed no opinion, not knowing what might have passed between you, and fearing to do more harm than good. Not a syllable about elections.[114]

Having dispatched Stanley, the Queen now reverted to holiday mode. She lunched, wrote and painted and went on a drive, *taking our tea with us. It was very dusty & hot. The moon had risen, as we drove back, reflecting itself beautifully in the Lake.*[115]

Pilatus, from the lake. Watercolour by Queen Victoria, 3 September 1868

7 *Incognita – the Acid Test*

It was now three and a half weeks since the Queen had arrived in Lucerne, in the full glare of international publicity and hoping against hope that she would not be mobbed, that her incognita mantle would shelter her from being importuned and that the gloomy forecasts of pessimists such as Lord Stanley would be proved wrong.

Her hopes were fulfilled. As the Queen and her retinue anxiously scanned the British press – sent out daily, with an extra set for 6 August – they were probably relieved to find that the papers were not only exercising self-discipline by not hounding her but were calling on their readers to give her a break (couched, of course, in suitably flowery nineteenth-century prose). For instance, on the Queen's first day in Switzerland *The Spectator* came out with a blistering broadside:

> The Queen ... will, her subjects hope, benefit as much by her holiday as if she were the wife of any Member of Parliament. She will not benefit, however, if watched, and hunted, and criticised as her sons have lately been. The conduct of the British public, and particularly of the well-fed section of it, in this matter is utterly disgraceful to them, not only as independent citizens, but as worshippers of rank. If they must be flunkeys – and they must be, or they would cease to be British – let them show their flunkeyism by reverent regard for the Queen's wishes, and let Her Majesty enjoy Mount Pilate without a hundred opera-glasses directed on her face.

Before, during and after the journey to Switzerland, the British press followed her every move at a respectful distance, and throughout the holiday there were short factual bulletins on her comings and goings. Earlier mentions of her being fatigued gave way later to reports of improving health and spirits. Harmless enough, but the Queen would have preferred no reporting at all of her movements, except when she drafted a bulletin herself.

It was not all plain sailing during the first two weeks. A correspondent of the *Daily News* reported:

> For a day or two after her Majesty's arrival she was, I am told, too fatigued to take much exercise, and confined herself almost entirely to the grounds of the mansion, and when she was able to go beyond them she at first suffered a good

deal from the impertinent curiosity of the tourists staying here. Wherever she drove she was followed by crowds of people; and so intolerable did the nuisance become, that I am told it was on one occasion found necessary to engage beforehand, as for the Royal party, all the vehicles in Lucerne in order that the public might be deprived of any means of transport. Whether in consequence of this hint, or as the result of greater familiarity with the presence of royalty, I know not; but her Majesty is now allowed to drive about the neighbourhood without being exposed to this kind of unpleasant intrusion.

Another correspondent noted that '... we have here a number of our own country people and Americans, who may be very 'distinguished', but do not look so.' Back in July Sir Thomas Biddulph had said 'what I fear most is tourists – mostly Americans.'[116] Events seemed to bear him out, as reported in *The Court Journal* at the end of August:

The Americans are, it seems, particularly desirous of seeing the Queen, and they pester Britishers with all manner of inquiries about her Majesty, the best means of approaching her, &c. One Briton, bored with questions from a Yankee lady, put it to her how he could be expected to satisfy her curiosity when all his personal knowledge of his august Sovereign was confined to seeing her drive in the park occasionally (he spoke of the days in which the Queen went into the park), and that he knew no more of her Majesty's household arrangements than he had been able to collect from contemplating the outside of Buckingham Palace. At this the Yankee lady evidently felt that she had been talking to a fellow who was nobody; and really she had reason to regret her loss of time, seeing that in any half dozen or other Englishmen she might have found two or three at least, who, judging from the manner in which they talked, were her Majesty's most intimate friends, and were going to Lucerne on her express invitation. But, overcoming her annoyance at conversing with so humble an individual, the fair Yankee cried, 'Well! I never saw a Queen, and of all Queens I am most anxious to see Queen Victoria! Tell me, at least, how I can recognise her Majesty if I should happen to meet her out of doors.' 'If you see a lady clad simply in black, driving in an open carriage, with two young ladies with her, and another carriage following, you will probably have the Queen and the Princesses, her daughters, before you!' 'A Queen like an ordinary lady! Well, I can't realise that anyhow!'

Sir Thomas need not have worried. As it turned out, that was as far as people got. *The Lady's Own Paper* wrote reassuringly that 'the great people are not mobbed'. And even that notorious sceptic Lord Stanley had to admit that there was 'an absence of population' around the Queen.[117] This also applied to any notables who might have hoped to call on the Queen. No 'incognita-crashing' for them, although there would have been quite a parade: amongst those holidaying in Lucerne at the time were the Count of Flanders, brother of the King of the Belgians, Charlotte, the widowed Empress of Mexico (herself prudently incognita), Archduke Henry of

Austria, to say nothing of French, Austrian and Bavarian ministers and no less than three Rothschilds. Queen Victoria's incognita kept them all at bay.

As for the Swiss, the Queen made an almost universally favourable impression on them. There was the initial unpleasantness over the noise from the bowling-alley near the pension and the republican rumblings occasioned by her monopolizing all the available accommodation on the Furka. But apart from that, what particularly struck the Swiss wherever she and her suite went was the Royal visitors' 'simple apparel' and 'modest comportment'. If anything they regretted the speed at which she was in and out of the places she went to. One who brilliantly met this problem head-on and overcame it (rather too spectacularly) as the Queen passed through Basle on her way to Lucerne achieved notoriety in a local newspaper:

> ... the keeper of the buffet at the railway station charged Queen Victoria and a suite of 30 persons 700 francs for a breakfast of coffee, eggs, and cold meat, being at the rate of 23 francs a head. The Bâle people are very indignant at this extortion, but the *restaurateur* would probably justify himself as the English innkeeper did who presented George III with a bill of one guinea for a slice of bread and one egg. The King, while paying the money, observed that eggs must be very scarce in that part of the country. 'No, Your Majesty,' was the reply, 'eggs are plentiful enough, but king's visits are rare.'

Such cases will have been infrequent. The Swiss always knew how to turn an honest penny, but they were seldom as rapacious as some indignant foreign travellers made out. They gave value for money. The Lucerne steamship company from whom the *Winkelried* was chartered were at great pains to do the right thing, even disarmingly writing to the British Legation in Berne for enlightenment:

> ... we have been given orders for preparing English flags for the use of our steamers. However there have been several different opinions as to the colour & design. We don't know a better authority to apply to than Her Majesty's Embassy. Would you be kind enough to inform us if we are right to cause the Flag to be made of red stuff with the well-known cross at the left corner – or ought the whole Flag to be filled up by the cross as we found on our 'Tableau des Pavillons' under the name of Jack. You would greatly oblige us in setting us right on this point![118]

The Legation answered immediately, 'giving some account of English flags in use.'

Some of the Queen's people at Lucerne developed a pronounced taste for Swiss beer, but there was a breakdown in communications when it came to paying. Three months after the Queen's departure the British Legation received a forlorn letter from the brewer, saying he no longer knew where to turn for payment of his invoice for a prodigious amount of beer, since he had received only Fr. 114 instead of the full amount of Fr. 174. A postscript pointed out that he had considered it a matter of honour to supply the best beer of his cellar to Her Majesty at Lucerne.

Recognition for the guide: testimonial, in A. Hofmann's leather-bound book

8 The Final Week

At the beginning of September the Queen, by now well rested and invigorated by her Alpine excursions – and who knows, perhaps even fortified by best Swiss beer – was ready to make full use of her remaining days in Switzerland. She began with another outing to Engelberg – to please the children, as she put it. It was not a great success.

> *September 2*
> *... The heat of the sun was very great & the dust most oppressive. It is an unpleasant tedious <u>nervous</u> road, so rough & narrow. Brown, who is always so attentive & watchful, got out & walked near the carriage, whenever we came to particularly steep & precipitous parts.*

They took lunch under the shade of some rocks and the Queen sketched, enjoying the view of the mountains, but they found the valley *'dreary'* and so

Rowing boat on lake. Watercolour by Queen Victoria, 3 September 1868

'*shut in*' that none of them cared for it much.[119] – However, they differ from the vast majority of visitors, who always find this valley the opposite of dreary.

After spending most of the next day in the summer house by the pension, the Queen took a turn on the lake, where she thought it would be cool and refreshing on the water, and made the only visit of the holiday to a private house. This stood on a lakeside promontory called Hertenstein at the foot of the Rigi and belonged to a leading local family which was later to provide the honorary British Vice-Consul in Lucerne.

Ponsonby, writing to his wife about that evening, conveys an atmosphere of jollity that says much for the curative powers of Switzerland. The Queen was laughing heartily again.

> Tonight at dinner Jenner gave us his account of his expedition up the Rigi with Bauer.* I don't know why my remarks are supposed always to be facetious when they are not. I simply asked what the tourists thought of their relationship. He replied oh of course they thought she was Madame which created some laughter. Then he added the guide was very decided and made us give up the horses we rode up – and come down in a chair. 'What?' I asked 'Both in one chair' – Well there is nothing odd in that but everyone laughed then I turned to Mary Bids – she was purple. On the other side I tried to speak to Louise She was choking. I looked across to Jenner. He was convulsed. Of course this was too much I gave way – we all had a fou rire till the tears ran down my cheeks which set off the Queen. I never saw her laugh so much. She said afterwds it was my face. At last we got a pause when Jane to set things strait again began with 'Did you find it comfortable?' which started us off again. My laugh was at Jenner stuffing his napkin over his mouth to stop himself at Mary Bids shaking and speechless on my side, and at Bids' solemn face.[120]

The full-day excursion that followed took the Queen, Princess Louise, Jane Ely and Colonel Ponsonby south to the Brünig Pass, reached by way of a long and obviously enjoyable drive.

> *September 4*
> *The valley here is very wide & much cultivated. Next reached Sarnen, a pretty picturesque village, & the very lovely Lake of Sarnen, which is long, much reminding one of the Scotch Lochs in the West Highlands. Towering mountains rise, as one drives along the lake. Came to Sachseln,*

---

* Fräulein Bauer, Princess Beatrice's governess, large and of limited charm.

another small town, where we changed horses. By this time it had become overpoweringly hot. At Giswyl, the next small place, people offered us milk, water & fruit. The road then began to get very steep & we ascended the Kaiserstuhl, soon after which we came to Lungern, another pretty picturesque village, where many tourists & carriages were waiting. The pretty, long Lake of Lungern soon came in sight & after that commences the long Brunnig Pass, which is splendid, high bold rocks, with silver fir growing up into the rocks & along the road, which is extremely good, & was only finished 7 years ago. The Wetterhorn with its snowy peaks, suddenly burst upon us, at the top of the Kaiserstuhl. At the beginning of the Brunnig Pass 3 little girls walked by the carriage singing very prettily in parts. At 1/4 to 2 we reached the top of Pass, but had no time to go further. However from here one could see the Engelshörner, very curiously formed, peaked mountains, – the Faulhorn, the Wendelhorn, Zelgerhorn, & Willhorn, a small portion of the Rosenlaui Gletscher, the Wetterhorn & Plattenstock.

The guide Hofmann had done an excellent job of instructing the Queen in the names of the various mountains and in locating them, and she was clearly an apt pupil. It was standard practice for travellers to toss off the names of mountains at every opportunity, rather like a litany.

September 5
Breakfast out & writing in the summer house. – Settled to go to Selisberg in the afternoon. Lunched a little earlier & started afterwards in 2 carriages with our 3 children, Janie E. & Col. Ponsonby, for the steamer, taking our ponies & 2 hired horses on board with us. Steamed to Treib, where there are only a few cottages & here we landed. The road was dreadfully bad, a steep climb up a <u>paved</u> road with occasional steps, of a slipperiness not to be described. Poor dear 'Flora' went beautifully, but it made me feel very nervous. It took us 3/4 of an hour going up. At the top there are 2 Hotels, which were full of curious odd

Showing the tortuous road from Treib to Seelisberg

The Final Week

people, & 2 Churches. The view is fine, overlooking the Lake, & the mountains to be seen: the Frotenalp, the Nieder Ober Bauenstock, the fine Uri Rothstock, with its glacier, to which we seemed quite close, the Breitenstock, the Windgellen & above the Tell's Platte the Axenberg. We again bought some wooden things, which I always give as souvenirs, to those who accompany us. Got off & walked some way, riding again a little, but when it came to a particularly steep part, I preferred being carried in a chaise à porteur, which the men, who are daily in the habit of it, did very carefully.

This is how the Queen would have been carried down the steepest part of the Seelisberg

Writing to Princess Victoria, the Queen confided that she did not much like being carried down: '*it is a humiliating proceeding*'.[121]

… September 5
We met several ladies being carried up & much luggage on men's backs, also one poor dog carrying heavy packs. The sun set splendidly & Pilatus & the Schwytzer Mythen, were beautifully lit up in the Alpenglühen. It was late when we got down to the bottom & steamed off, as quick as we

Schwyzer Mythen. Watercolour by Queen Victoria, 5 September 1868

could. Had our tea on board, & only got home at 1/4p.8. – During dinner, the amateur singers of Lucerne serenaded us & very well. I went & thanked them afterwards, & while we were sitting gazing at the moonlit lake & landscape, they sang 2 songs with Yodeln. –

September 6
Fine, but very hot. – Breakfast out & writing till 12, when Mr. Duckworth held a short service. – Directly afterwards Louise & I made sketches of a girl from Engelberg. – Drove in the afternoon with Louise, & sketched in a field where we took our tea, a beautiful view of Pilatus. – Sitting out after dinner. –

The next morning the Queen wrote at length to Disraeli on the episcopal appointment to be made. And Jane Ely sat down to write Disraeli (at the Queen's request) a letter in which she was at pains to explain the logic behind recent dramatic developments in the Paris visit saga.

The situation had indeed been changing with bewildering speed. To begin with, there had been a Prussian outflanking manoeuvre launched soon after the Queen had agreed to visit the Empress in Paris. Jane Ely reported it immediately.

Woman in Unterwalden costume.
Watercolour sketch by Queen Victoria

I am going to tell you a <u>little secret</u> [she wrote to Stanley on 3 September, with her punctuation letting her down even more than usual], which you must kindly keep for me as it is not even spoken of in the house. The Queen has heard from the Princess Royal of Prussia, that The Queen (Dowg)* is coming here, incognito, and the Queen intends to pay her Majesty a private visit as The Queen says she feels sure it will please and have a good effect in Prussia, I am sure it will and please them immensely. The Queen thinks it will do away with any bad effect, of the visit to Paris, I tell you this my dear Lord Stanley, because I mentioned

---

* The Princess Royal, i.e. Crown Princess Victoria, was referring to her aunt-in-law, the Dowager Queen Elisabeth of Prussia.

to you the other day, the Queen's dread lest what she did in Paris might create jealousy elsewhere. The Queen told me this yesterday, but told me not to mention it, in the household, as The Queen wished it kept quiet, but I feel you will like to know it and also know you will not mention it.[122]

Stanley was a man of honour. He waited a day before telling the Prime Minister. Meanwhile he confided to his diary his reaction to this cunning move from the north: *I hear from Ly Ely, privately, that the Queen, after having announced her intention to see no one at Lucerne, has now settled to receive a visit from the Queen of Prussia: that is, from the one person whose coming will be most distasteful to the French government.*[123]

Then, in his letter to Disraeli, Stanley showed that this new source of pressure on the Queen was making him see her behaviour in a new light. 'I hear on good authority that German, and especially Darmstadt influence has been at work to limit as far as possible the exchange of civilities at Paris, and that the refusal in the first instance was not the result of accident or whim, but predetermined.'[124]

There was more to tell in this letter:

> All wrong again – but this time not by the Countess's fault. She agreed to call on Eugénie in Paris: now the latter objects to come up, and wishes the visit to take place at Fontainebleau – that is, in the early morning, after a night in the train, and after making a long road to get there. This the Queen will not do, and I really don't think she could be expected to do it. The original fault of the non-returned visit remains, but in the subsequent proceedings we have got ourselves in the right. The Empress will probably go off to Biarritz, and there the matter will end.[125]

So fate (with a little help from Prussia) was going to be kind to the Queen in Paris. Meanwhile, though, she had realized what she had let herself in for by agreeing so readily to the other visit (the one wished upon her by her kin in Germany), to the Dowager Queen of Prussia in Lucerne. She had first written to the Crown Princess that

> I should much like to see her and think that I could manage to do it – if you would let me know the exact day of her arrival. I could manage to <u>go quite</u> privately <u>in my drive</u> to see her. Her case is really exceptional, and perhaps they would not put it into the German papers nor would I have it put into the English Court Circular.[126]

Three days later she was in a mood to call this visit off, having heard that the Dowager Queen would only arrive in Lucerne on the day of her own departure and having had time to reflect on other implications. 'As the Dwr. Queen only arrives on the 9th I cannot go & see her, & it wld be best to explain that,' she wrote to the Crown Princess. '– Indeed as I have had some trouble with the Empr. & Empss of the F. it wld be better I shld not go to see her – as it wld leak out.'[127]

A day later Prussia was on again but Paris was off.

This, then, was the state of affairs which the Queen was now asking Lady Ely to lay before the Prime Minister, who might by now have been more than somewhat confused by the zig-zag march of events. Taking a deep breath, she bravely set to, her anxiety to explain and justify rather at odds with the length of her sentences.

> You will no doubt have heard ere this, that The Queen's visit to the Empress cannot take place. The Queen said she really could not stop at Fontainebleau on her way to Paris, that Her Majesty had been invited by the Grand Duke and Duchess of Baden, if the Queen changed her route, to rest for a night in a Palace belonging to them, & The Queen had declined saying she went no where. The Queen desires me to tell you, that Her Majesty has written to the Empress herself, to express all her regrets, but to say, Her Majesty had given up paying visits now, & had declined going to her own relations, but hoped at some future time, when she passed through Paris to call & see The Empress. I am sure that the Queen's letter will go far to allay any soreness that is felt. The Queen has been much troubled about it, she showed me your letter to her & said you had written so kindly & nicely. The Queen also desires me to say to you, Her Majesty had desired the Morning Post should not put in articles or notices about Her Majesty's movements, & they had promised only to insert what was sent to them by Her Majesty's orders; since the Queen has been here, they have not adhered to that promise & Her Majesty would be so much obliged to you, if you could have something done about it, to prevent the repetition of this annoyance, to the Queen. ... She is very sorry to give you so much trouble. ... The Queen always speaks of you in the kindest & nicest manner & is constantly saying how considerate you are & that you understood her.[128]

The prospect of losing Disraeli if the Conservatives were defeated in the coming election must have clouded the Queen's enjoyment of her holiday, but being a constitutional and not an absolute monarch she was conditioned to a certain degree of reticence where party politics were concerned. A more immediate anxiety, of course, was to keep her forthcoming meeting with the Prussian Queen from leaking out and putting herself and her country in the dog-house as far as the French were concerned.

She now had only three days left in Switzerland and was determined to make the most of them. Ponsonby was going around singing the praises of a little-known church he had discovered not far from Lucerne. He had written to his wife about it:

> I drove with Duckworth and P. Leopold this afternoon to my favourite little drive of Herrgotteswald. I have taken everyone there now except the Queen. It is only about 1 1/2 hours off. Thick woods, a deep ravine high hills & in front Pilate rising grandly before you. An ascent of a wooden staircase about 1000 steps or more brings you to the church. Most curious. The whole ceiling covered with crests or mottoes. Really good figures of about 20 saints etc. But the views magnificent. Pr'aps I've told you all this before. But I am always full of it – & there is nothing in the guide books about it, & the guides don't know it.[129]

Now Ponsonby talked the Queen into going to see for herself.

> *September 7*
> *The time for going away, is fast approaching. – ... In the afternoon drove with Louise, Leopold & Janie E. to see a curious old Church below the Schwartzenberg, & in fact close to Pilatus, from whence the view was very fine. After we had gone a little way beyond Reuzlach we stopped & got on our ponies. Rode through one of those curious covered bridges, overlooking a ravine. Gradually the path became very steep & slippery & I got off & walked, but it was very trying, as I am a bad climber & had not tried it for 6 years. The view of Pilatus on one side & of the lake below was perfectly beautiful. Passed a sort of farm house, below which stands the curious old Church Herrgotteswald. We walked down to &*

From Herrgotteswald.
Sketch by Princess Louise,
7 September 1868

Drawing by Queen Victoria, 7 September 1868. She captioned it: *'Ach geben Sie mir ein kleines boutönchen oder so etwas'* (Spare a copper, lady).
Since her bereavement, the Queen had hardly sketched people, but only places. Here was a sign that she was recovering some of her old verve

into it. Then looked about for a place to take our tea, & found one just above a small inn. Here Louise & I afterwards sketched a little. The Alpenglühen was again very lovely but very quickly over. Began our descent, Brown helping me & holding me up, else I should have never succeeded in getting down over that bad ground, my knees being very weak & rheumatic. When we came to the bend, remounted my pony & rode on to where the carriage was waiting. It was fast getting dark, & we made Benz drive quickly home. – Sitting out after dinner. –

September 8
The sun very hot. – Breakfast out & sitting writing in that nice summer house. – Settled to go out early, alas! for the last time, for it is sad to be leaving such beautiful scenery, though I shall be glad to go to my own dear Highland home.

Two days earlier the Queen had already written to Princess Victoria in similar vein: 'I shall remain the 12th and 13th at Windsor & start on the night of the 14th for dear Balmoral where I shall be glad to be again on account of the air & the quiet & the dear people whom one misses shockingly here.'[130]

Yet it almost looks as if in spite of this the Queen was finding it difficult to tear herself away from Switzerland. This excursion was to be the last, but in the event she took two more 'last' drives the day after, right up to her departure in the evening. Gone were all those earlier pleas of exhaustion and malaise that had so bedevilled the earlier part of her holiday.

… September 8
Started after luncheon with Baby, Janie E. & Mary B. for the steamer,

steaming up to Brunnen. It all looked so beautiful, that the thought of no longer seeing that glorious scenery made one quite sad. We landed and got into our carriage, which we had brought with us. It was a holiday, many of the peasant women being out in their smart costumes. Drove a short way along the Axenstrasse and then turned up a totally new road, safe & good, though very steep. It was beautiful, under splendid rocks & through fine fir trees, & gradually the most glorious view of the Lake & mountains opened out. Came to the small village of Marschach, close under the highest points of the Fronnalp, with Châlets, trees & valleys, one of the finest spots we have yet been to. It took us an hour to get up to the very top of this road, where a large Hotel is being built, & where the air is beautiful. Got out for a moment to gaze at the magnificent view, which was perfectly clear, the sun setting over Pilatus, but unfortunately we could not wait to see it actually go down, as darkness comes on so quickly, without hardly any twilight. Got down easily & at once got on board the steamer & steamed off, taking our tea, as we went. It was quite dark by the time we got back, though very starlight, & Lucerne looked extremely pretty lit up. – Some singers again came to serenade us whilst we were at dinner.

Now came the day of departure.

September 9
Breakfast out & then took a lovely drive with Louise, our last, *along the beautiful lake, through the town, & back by the Kreuzbuche. So glad to get the last & most beautiful view of all the mountains, in the soft vapoury morning light, all so clear. – Took another little drive in the afternoon & when I came back gave Hoffmann a pin with my cypher & Bentz also a pin, he making me a speech of thanks, also for taking his daughter Elise or Lisele to England as housemaid. She has been acting as such here & was good & active. – At 1/4 to 7 we left with* real *regret the dear comfortable, cheerful little home of Pension Wallis, where we had spent quiet & very pleasant days, & where all had lived like a family together. Drove with our 3 Children down to the station & waited a few moments in the waiting room, where I saw the Dowager Queen of Prussia whom I had not seen for 23 years, when all was bright & happy for us both & our dear Husbands were well, & my beloved one so young! They were both taken the same year! The Queen is grown very old but I should have known her again, & she was most kind. She had expressed such a wish to see me, that she had offered, though only just arrived at Lucerne, to come up to see me this afternoon, but the house was in too great a state of confusion to allow of that.*

A railway station was – to put it mildly – not quite the place for such a meeting. The Queen knew it and was at pains to explain it away to the Crown Princess:

> She only arrived in the afternoon but <u>most</u> kindly shewed so much wish to see me – that she offered to come up, or to meet me at the Station, & as our little Home with <u>all</u> the packages carrying out by the <u>only door</u>, was totally <u>unfit</u> for her to come to – I agreed to the latter. She was so very kind & herzlich that I was much touched by it.[131]

> *... September 9*
> *I only remained about 10 minutes talking, while everything was being got ready, & then entered the train, taking leave of good Hoffmann from the window of the saloon.*

IN FRANCE – EN ROUTE BACK HOME

It was Emperor Napoleon III's saloon train, the same as on the outward journey, that was now rattling its way towards Paris on the way back. But whereas then, in early August, the Queen had not been able to sleep at all, now she '*got a good deal of sleep during the night*',[132] and Lady Ely wrote to Disraeli from the British Embassy, where they spent the day, that the Queen '*seems ... not in the least tired after her journey*'.[133]

But the heat of the city, and probably the prospect of having to return to everyday life, gave her a headache, which was not made better by her going on a sentimental journey to the Palace of St Cloud where she had stayed on her triumphal visit in 1855.

> *September 10*
> *At 1/2 p. 5, after taking tea, drove out in Ld. Lyons' carriage, with him, Louise & Janie E., the 2 Children with Frl. Bauer & Col. Ponsonby, following in another carriage. We went through the Champs Elysées, past the Arc de Triomphe, which I recognised well, through the Bois de Boulogne, which looked dull & dreary at this time of year, – through the small town of Boulogne, – over the bridge to St. Cloud, which I much wished to look at again, in remembrance of the happy days spent there with my dearest Albert in 55. Drove into the quadrangle, where we stopped for a moment at the door, but being tired, & having little time I did not get out. Besides, the idea of seeing those rooms again, now uninhabited & triste, would have been too painful for me. But I*

recognised all & was able to look through the open door at the great Staircase, where there is now a picture, representing our arrival in 55. Drove round the garden, which looked bright, but the fine avenues & silent house made a very dreary & sad impression upon me. It was dull, hazy & oppressive.

Back at the Embassy, she complained that

a Café Chantant, at the end of the garden, outside, made such a noise that I could get no rest. Such a contrast, to the quiet little house at Lucerne.- Dined alone with Louise. The room opened on to the garden, & the fountain made it pleasant & look cool. Started at 10 for Cherbourg, Ld. Lyons accompanying us to the station.[134]

A day in Paris had left the Queen's incognita distinctly frayed at the edges. In the afternoon her every move – even the way she looked through the windows of St Cloud during her visit there – had been closely followed by the press, albeit with benevolent eyes. *Galignani's Messenger* wrote:

Her Majesty was so greatly affected that she could not enter the apartments, and remained for some time at the entrance. It was merely through the windows that the Royal visitor cast a look full of tenderness on those rooms which she had occupied so happily in company with the Prince Consort during their visit to Paris. The Queen walked in the gardens, but still, from time to time, glanced at the interior.

Nothing highlights the contrast between the simplicity of Switzerland and the pomp of Paris better than the spectacular arrangements for her departure, cordial though they were. Her departure in the evening as duly reported in *La Presse* and relayed later in *The Times*,[135] could almost have passed for the end of a full-blown State Visit; only the flowers and the Imperial Family were missing.

The St. Lazare station changed its physiognomy during two hours of Thursday evening. The arrival quays of the Normandie Line were enlarged and carpeted, as was also the great waiting room that communicates with the court of exit. The rooms and the line were brilliantly lighted up. A special train, composed of the Emperor's saloon carriage and of ten first-class carriages with luggage vans, kept its steam up in the middle of the line. The company's chief officers, in black coats and white cravats, were there collected, the Secretary-General replacing the director, who is away from Paris. Those officials who were to go on duty with the train were all in full dress, as was also Dr. Bergier, the company's chief physician, who took his seat in a carriage with his instruments and medicaments. At half-past 9 the persons composing the suite of the Queen of England began to occupy the places assigned to them by the majordomo. Soon afterwards a closed landau and pair brought her Britannic Majesty, her two daughters and her son Leopold to the entrance of the large waiting room. The Ambassador's carriage followed. The Queen, preceded by a chamberlain of her Court, advanced first towards the imperial train, surrounded by her family; the English Ambassador followed, bareheaded. There was profound silence; all the persons who had been admitted into the station took off their hats. The Queen wore a black dress and a black lace bonnet. Everybody remarked the simplicity of her attire and the modesty of her attitude. Out of respect for the Queen's mourning and her incognita, the railway administration had not put flowers in the station as is generally done at the departure of Sovereigns. The Queen got into the carriage first, without any assistance. The two young Princesses and the Prince followed, and the chamberlain shut the door. Lord Lyons stood at the door of the waggon, hat in hand, on the side on which his Sovereign was seated. The Princess Louise, who was opposite to the Queen, exchanged a few words with the Ambassador. When the whistle sounded for the departure, the august traveller waved her hand to Lord Lyons, who bowed low, and the train started at full steam on the line for Cherbourg. ... On Friday morning at 6.30, the train reached the military port of Cherbourg, where the Queen left the railway for a yacht, which was like leaving one apartment for another, the arrangements there being admirably adapted for the transition.

The Queen's day in Paris had seen the dénouement of the long drawn-out drama that had developed out of her famous refusal to return Empress Eugénie's call when she first passed through Paris in August. After all those weeks of recrimination, cajoling and manoeuvring, the Queen – having finally been cornered into agreeing to return the call on her way back – now managed to turn the tables on her tormentors and avoid making the call after all. With great tactical skill she had lulled the opposition into a false sense of security when outnumbered at Lucerne, bided her time and was then saved from an unexpected quarter: the Empress for various reasons found herself unable to be in Paris on the day the Queen was there. The whole business ended with an exchange of friendly messages. Although Queen Victoria had risked a worsening of Anglo-French relations by meeting the Dowager Queen of Prussia in Lucerne at the last moment, she had managed to keep this meeting from leaking out. For the Queen it was victory on all fronts: she had done the decent thing by her German relatives, she was discreetly fostering diplomatic relations with Prussia without at the same time jeopardizing those with France and she was off the hook in Paris, spared having to make a formal visit.

So honour was in the end satisfied and the Queen set sail for England not only refreshed by her month in Switzerland but victorious in her dealings with her Ministers and diplomats.

On 11 September 1868 *The Times* had another leading article (to match that of 7 August) to celebrate the Queen's return to her realm and round off her stay in Switzerland.

LONDON, FRIDAY, SEPTEMBER 11, 1868

The stream of returning tourists has this year a splendid addition. Queen VICTORIA has had the enterprise and the good sense to see what every one of her subjects sees if he can, and has accomplished a few of the most familiar, most accessible, and, it may be added, most beautiful objects in Switzerland. In so doing she has put an end to one reflection which rises to everybody's lips in the grandest spots of a progress through that country. It is a thought of pity for Royalty that, whatever it may see in palaces, parks, and Scotch Highlands, it cannot see Switzerland. The clerk or the curate scrapes up his 50£ and forgets his cares in Switzerland; the newly married couple, the master of a small competency, the father of the daughters to be brought out in the world, the elderly folk released from ties, and the solitary cast on the world, all meet there, and are in heaven for a time. Small people become great people, and great people small, once on their legs, or on mountain horses, or asking admission to crowded hotels a good mile above the clouds, or seeking a place at the dinner-table, or inquiring for a guide. There is no such happiness in this sublunary sphere – indeed, it is not felt to be sublunary, and in that rarefied atmosphere even extortions, mistakes, and long bills are soon forgotten. The struggle to rise, which takes a lifetime in England, and is not there achieved without many downfalls, takes a few hours, and by noon, if you are early enough, the world lies below your feet. Thence, after a brief rest, an easy descent to dinner and bed. Tomorrow you resume. Every day the traveller sees as many of his fair, intelligent, or well-to-do compatriots as he is likely to see in a twelvemonth in a country seat or a country town. Learning is there an involuntary process and memory indelible. It is impossible not to notice and to remember. The stream of life is human, and therefore with the usual well-known drawbacks of humanity, but it is a little disguised. It is the world in a grand picnic, mankind glorified in a mountain ballet. Nature somewhat diminishes the scale of life, and tones down even the strong features of the Great Briton. But how could we subsist so many centuries without Switzerland? This mitigation of our sad insular lot was only discovered, one may say, about fifty years ago; but since that it has become a necessity. The SOVEREIGN was the only one in the realm denied the common joy. There are those who affirm, believe, and certainly feel that the mountains of Scotland, not to say of Wales and of the Lakes, are superior to those of Switzerland in beauty of form and colour; that they excel in the shades of the foliage and in the lights of the atmosphere; that the air of a Scotch valley is purer than that of a Swiss. But, nevertheless, even with that horrid sea to cross and recross, and with a thousand miles to be done between this and the Alps, costing 25£ a head the move to and fro, our people still turn their steps to Switzerland with an instinct as common and irresistible as that which directs a shoal of herrings or half the birds of this island in their annual migrations.

The conditions of Royalty have prevented what is called a tour, and have confined HER MAJESTY to a few points within reach of Lucerne. But the selection has been judicious, and the QUEEN has been enabled to see some things that everybody has seen, some things that very few have seen, and fair specimens of every kind of Swiss scenery. Everybody knows the quaint mediaeval city of Lucerne, its marvellous and almost too scenic combination of lakes, and the Righi, which is pretty nearly all Switzerland and a good deal more at one view, the beautiful ascent of the St. Gothard road, the lofty desolation of the Furka Pass, the huge glaciers of the Rhone, and the innumerable objects comprised in these titles. But very few have visited Engelberg and the ascents of the Tittlis, said to have no equal in beauty. Very few comparatively go up Pilatus, though a much grander mountain than the Righi, and commanding, if not so extensive a view, yet one more sublime and purely Alpine than that from the Righi Culm. Lucerne is the only point where so many various objects of interest are within easy reach, and where life would be very tolerable even if the weather should prevent mountaineering. The loyal regret, or the disloyal self-gratulation, will still return at a few other points of that charmed region. There are Grindelwald and Chamounix, the upper end of the Lake of Geneva, the Gemmi, the Grimsel, Zermatt, and the eastern mountains and valleys of Switzerland, where the most inveterate tourists are now finding grander and more picturesque scenery than any they saw before. There is the one view of Mont Blanc from the summit of the old diligence road from Dôle, whence the mountain, fifty miles off, is seen in the skies, and the intervening Lake of Geneva far below one's feet. But it is necessary to tear one's self away from the well-remembered scenes. The QUEEN is still young, happily strong, and with sufficient enterprise. She may return to Switzerland another year. Her subjects, who feel an intense and inexhaustible curiosity to know or imagine how anything strikes the eye of Royalty, will amuse themselves for some time in speculating whether Scotland holds her own against Switzerland, whether outline and colour tell against bulk, or whether eternal snow has the same fascination for Sovereigns as for citizens. We believe it to be almost everybody's experience that the great upper land of Europe, midway between nations and the sky, and the very paradise whence spring north, south, and east the three great rivers of the continent, is a new creation, and brings a new nature, if it may be said, to every mind at all open to new impressions. It is a return to youth; a new start in life and feeling, a softening of the past, a brightening of the future, and the opening of fresh springs of feeling and of thought.

Well, HER MAJESTY has had this rare fortune for Sovereigns, so common to even the "lower middle" class of her drudging and generally stay-at-home subjects. We confess ourselves well pleased that her circle should be widened, and that she should see more than is visible in a periodical oscillation between Osborne and Balmoral. Anything to interrupt an inveterate habit and break the spell of sorrowful and saddening recollections. Why else were these marvels of creation given us, these glimpses of a new heaven and a new earth! There are few, if any, who do not require, at least once in their lives, to have the train of thought turned by some sweet violence into a more practical and salutary direction. Since new duties cannot be made, or new persons started into existence, new scenes are the appointed method, and no balm is more soothing or effective. Often and often are returning tourists found to aver they do not come home rested in body, or certainly better in physical health; but that in the fund of new impressions and the passing away of old troubles they feel the certainty of returning health and strength and a new lease of vitality. Having thrown herself, with a laudable effort, into the great European stream of tourists, even for a few days, the QUEEN will feel herself once more in the living, moving world. There, in the presence of a more than human majesty, and in a court higher than that of any earthly realm, she has seen a gathering of all nations assembled to offer at least the secret service of their souls. It is an occasion and a spectacle to open the heart long locked in private contemplation, to revive the sympathies, and to reduce to its due proportion everything that is exaggerated and engrossing. The QUEEN now shares with her subjects many of the grandest recollections that nature can supply, and that can at once elevate and bring into unison the souls of all that have them. In this way she is more at home with us, and a sharer of thoughts and pleasures almost domestic in their character. She has felt that touch of Alpine nature which makes us all kin. The beauties of Switzerland are household words in this country, and at every fireside where they are known and remembered the Royal tourist will now be, in thought, a fellow-traveller and self-invited guest.

PART
Three

9 *Aftermath*

The Queen was clearly the better for this Swiss interlude – perhaps more than she realized, or indeed admitted to herself. True, it had not wrought a miracle cure for her nerves or for her underlying state of mind; some years were to elapse before she finally found the strength and inner balance that enabled her to crown her long reign with thirty years of glory. Yet this first break with her recent past did initiate a change.

She was now finally emerging from the depths of her mourning. She had had the complete change and quiet she had been seeking for so long, as well as the stimulus of excursions to places far and wide. She had not needed to be at odds with the outside world – indeed there had been no conceivable cause (except, for a few days, the weather). Affairs of state had been routine, hardly anything contentious, apart from ecclesiastic appointments and of course the great Paris visit fracas. She had ventured into a totally new environment where in a close family circle she could be herself, untrammelled by Court ritual or public pressure. Whether or not the seeds of her later reconciliation to her fate were sown during these both peaceful and stimulating weeks, they will have given her a gentle kick-start for a new phase in her life. Henceforth her desolation was less settled than it had been.

Meanwhile, it was back to everyday life. Once she stepped ashore at Portsmouth on 11 September after crossing the Channel, the Countess of Kent became the Queen of England again. A brief stay at Windsor plunged her back into the thick of public affairs. On arrival she found a letter from Disraeli, the grandiloquent flourish with which it begins barely concealing his anxiety to get the Queen back to business as usual: 'He begs permission to offer his humble congratulations to Yr. Majesty on Yr. Majesty's return to Yr. Majesty's dominions, & trusts, & believes, that the visit to Lucerne will have given tone both to the spirit, & the frame, of Yr. Majesty, & will always be remembered with salutary gratification.'[136] Disraeli then 'proposes to avail himself of Yr. Majesty's most gracious permission to be in audience of Yr. Majesty on Sunday next, at three o'clock, as there are matters of great moment to be submitted to Yr. Majesty & the Council Day wd. be scarcely convenient for that purpose.'[137]

These were matters he had not wanted to bother the Queen with at Lucerne, particularly the politically sensitive appointment of a new Bishop of Peterborough. Being a past master in the art of combining flattery with cajolery, he had taken the precaution of broaching the subject in a letter to the Queen just after she had returned to Lucerne from her stay on the Furka pass:

> Mr. Disraeli with his humble duty to your Majesty ... He is sincerely gratified, that the expedition to the Furca was successful. It is a great thing to have seen the glacier of the Rhone; greater to have walked upon it. This visit alone would repay your Majesty for much exertion and some suffering. When these are passed and forgotten, the recollection of beautiful and striking scenery remains; and adds to the aggregate of those pleasing memories, that make life interesting ... Since Mr. Disraeli wrote last to your Majesty, a long impending vacancy in the Episcopal Bench has occurred. There is no necessity to precipitate the appointment, and the final decision can await your Majesty's return ... On the nomination to the see of Peterborough in the present temper of the country, much depends ...[138]

Now at Windsor, the very next day after this private audience with Disraeli, the Queen held a Council at which it was decided to prorogue Parliament further until 26 November. The Queen was in the thick of formality again and the Court Circular for 14 September reflected it:

> The United States' Minister arrived at the Castle this afternoon, and was introduced to Her Majesty by Lord Stanley, Secretary of State for Foreign Affairs, and presented his credentials.
> Her Majesty held a Council this afternoon at 3 o'clock, at which were present the Duke of Marlborough, the Right Hon. Benjamin Disraeli, the Earl of Devon, Lord Stanley, and the Judge-Advocate-General.
> Previous to the Council the Duke of Marlborough and the Judge-Advocate-General had audiences of Her Majesty.
> Mr. Helps was Clerk of the Council.
> Viscount Bridport and Colonel Du Plat, Equerries in Waiting, were in attendance.
> The Queen, accompanied by Princess Louise, Prince Leopold, and Princess Beatrice, left the Castle this evening at a quarter before 7 o'clock for Balmoral.

The journey north – with the immensely long Royal train occupied by a powerful contingent of the Royal Household – was a far cry indeed from the simple style the Queen had been keeping in Switzerland. It was reported in *The Times* in meticulous detail.

> Her Majesty, on quitting the Castle, drove to the Windsor station of the Great Western Railway, where Prince and Princess Christian of Schleswig-Holstein and Prince Christian Victor had arrived. The public having, by the courtesy of the railway authorities, been admitted to the terminus, the platform was consequently thronged by a large assemblage of spectators, all of whom were attracted by the prospect of seeing the Queen leave for Scotland. Many arrived at the station early and remained a considerable time before the hour fixed for the Royal departure. There they passed the time by inspecting the special train with its handsome saloons fitted with sleeping appliances. The Royal train numbering some 14 carriages, had been despatched from the Euston station of the London and North-Western Railway under the care of Mr Bore, the superintendant of the carriage department, and reached Windsor shortly after 2 o'clock. Her Majesty and the Royal family on alighting at the Windsor station were received by the principal officers of the Great Western and London and North-Western Railways, and the illustrious travellers at once took their seats in the saloons. Her Majesty and Princess Louise occupied the Royal saloon, which was placed in about the centre of the train and was the seventh vehicle from the engine. Prince and Princess Christian, with Prince Christian Victor and the nurse, sat in a double saloon in front of the Queen, between which and that occupied by their Royal Highnesses was another double saloon, containing the Queen's personal servants and the dressers. Behind Her Majesty's saloon was one with her Royal Highness Princess Beatrice, governess, and maid, while the next to that contained Prince Leopold and his attendants. Sir T.M. Biddulph and Lord Bridport had the next saloon, the directors and Prince Christian's attendants riding in the adjoining carriages. The rear of the train was brought up by the Queen's fourgon and a break van. The rest of the carriages in front of the Royal saloons were allotted to Her Majesty's dressers, pages, and upper servants. The length of the Royal train was 401 ft., not including the engine, and the Queen's saloon and the other carriages were fitted throughout with Mr Martin's system of electrical communication between passengers and guards. The Royal train quitted the Windsor station at 6.50 p.m., under the care of Mr Tyrrell, the Superintendant of the Great Western line, Her Majesty's route being by way of Reading and Didcot to Oxford, where the train arrived at 8.6 p.m. A stay of 5 minutes was made here and at 8.11 the trip was resumed.[139]

And so on, right up to the Highlands, all stopping places with times reached and mileages (even fractions of a mile) being proudly set forth. Balmoral was reached at 2 p.m. the following afternoon.

During the Queen's autumn residence there, troubles both public and private once again beset her. There were Church appointments still to be made, with a government in pre-election mood looking at the political leanings of the candidates more than suited the Queen. There was the increasingly fearsome prospect of a General Election – not only the first since the Second Reform Bill of 1867, but one which might well sweep the Conservatives from office and her congenial Prime Minister Disraeli into the political wilderness, to be replaced by the far from congenial Gladstone. And there was all-round trepidation at the implications of Prince Alfred's determination to marry a Russian (or Greek as it was then called) Orthodox Princess – and the daughter of the Czar, Alexander II at that. Prince Alfred had in his way been a problem son before. Now he had come up with something that was not only a personal headache for the Queen, but a constitutional one for the government.

This had already been the subject of confidential correspondence during the Queen's stay in Switzerland. Sir Thomas Biddulph had written to Disraeli in early September: 'The Duke of Edinburgh, as is usually the case with young men in love, presses the Queen for an immediate answer.' There was apparently an early opportunity for the Czar and the Czarina to be asked whether Prince Alfred might become their daughter's suitor. The Queen wanted the government's opinion before letting this happen. 'It is certain,' Biddulph continued, 'that there is little choice of bride for the young Princes, and the Duke appears to have picked out this young lady for himself. If he could settle himself it would no doubt be a great point gained.'[140] This was a covering letter for a confidential memo written on behalf of the Queen.

Disraeli as a fox making up to Queen Victoria, with Gladstone sharpening his knife in the portrait behind. Cartoon by Richard Doyle

> The Queen has desired me to write to you very confidentially on a subject of great interest to Her Majesty, and of considerable political importance....
>
> Her Majesty has long wished that the Duke of Edinburgh might make a suitable marriage, but up to this time H.R.H. has shewn no disposition to form any allegiance. Within however the last few weeks, he has had the opportunity of meeting the Emperor of Russia and his family at Darmstadt. It appears both the Emperor & Empress have treated him with marked kinship, and the acquaintance he has made with their only daughter, the Grand Duchess Marie, has produced such an impression on his mind, that he asks the Queen's leave, before going abroad on his cruize, to request the Emperor & Empress to allow him to renew his acquaintance with their daughter on his return, and in short at that time to become a suitor for her hand. I should observe that the Grand

Duchess Marie is at present under 15 years of age, and that therefore some time must elapse before, under any circumstances, a marriage could take place, but the Duke fears that during his absence, should he leave without giving any intimation of his intentions, some other arrangement might be made.

The account which the Queen hears of the personal qualifications of the young Princess are very favourable, and on this score, Her Majesty has no reason whatever to object, but the question on which Her Majesty desires your opinion is whether the fact of the Grand Duchess belonging to the Greek Church would legally or politically present an insurmountable obstacle.[141]

This request stuck in the throat of the government, who saw various obstacles and put them to the Queen. As late as 5 October the Lord Chancellor expressed his concern that at this crisis time for the government a political act such as this should be taken by the Cabinet. 'English feeling is on such matters highly sensitive & highly uncertain. A section of our Church wd probably hail the alliance as a means of promoting the union of Churches which they have in view: & just in the same proportion it wd become unpalatable to another section.' In the end (in 1874) Prince Alfred married his chosen one, but only after a good deal more political and ecclesiastical agonizing.

As if the Queen had not had her fill of wrangling with Disraeli over Church appointments, now – quite unexpectedly – none other than the Archbishop of Canterbury died, which plunged the Queen yet again into a trial of wills concerning the nomination of his successor. She stuck to her guns and got her candidate through.

Foreign affairs also gave the Queen cause for concern soon after her return from Switzerland – not only as a mother with children in Germany, but as Queen of a country whose maxim of non-interference in Continental affairs was under growing strain. Belgium was feeling threatened and asked for a British guarantee of help if it was attacked by France. The Foreign Secretary, Lord Stanley, thought this should not be given. The Queen could not overrule this political position, but she had her own recipe and at the end of September instructed General Grey to convey it to Disraeli:

I have written by her command to the King of the Belgians stating Stanley's reasons for thinking such interference as the King asks for, would be inexpedient at the present moment at all events.

But Her Majesty does not think the Belgian govt. can be blamed for feeling suspicious of French designs. – A powerful party amongst French official men have never concealed their wish to effect the annexation of Belgium – and we cannot forget the readiness which Bismarck expressed, at one time at all events to assist that wish.

> It was to prevent the danger of a combination between France and Prussia to effect an object which, if attained, would be so fatally injurious to English Interests, that the Queen has always urged the expediency of making it clearly understood both at Paris and Berlin that England would never stand quietly by, & see the Independence of Belgium attacked. – She did not wish any official diplomatic action to be taken in the matter. – But there are always ways of letting a determination be known which are equally effective.[142]

The General Election in mid-November brought the expected swing in favour of the Liberals, who had a majority of about 120. The Queen recorded in her Journal on 23 November that the defeated Disraeli asked her '... *what did I wish them to do? Whatever he thought was the best, I answered*.[143]

Normal parliamentary practice would have been for the Prime Minister and his Cabinet to be ejected from office on the first meeting of the new Parliament. But in view of this decisive result, Disraeli created a precedent and resigned almost at once.

The Queen now had the – for her – unhappy task of sending for Gladstone and charging him to form a Cabinet. This brought with it the appalling prospect of having to deal with some of the people he might choose.

> ... she owns she is haunted by the fear of want of consideration from the new ones [she wrote to General Grey on 23 November]. She feels very depressed at the trials before her, but she will meet all except having people who are insolent and rude to her. She has only heard this evening from Princess Mary how insolent & bitter & even impertinent Lord Clarendon is. The Queen will not have him; she could not stand it. Another who the Queen would wish should not be brought in close contact with her & for whom she has a great personal aversion, for she knows him to be very sarcastic & unkind, is Mr Lowe. He must not be a Secretary of State. Anything short of this. Now tho' Mr Bright is very violent he has always shown the kindest feeling for the Queen & publicly on 2 occasions spoken very feelingly when the world spoke unfeelingly & ungently. The Queen is sure that Lord Halifax can do a great deal.[144]

Once the new Cabinet had been appointed, the great hand-kissing ceremony had to be got through. With Liberal zeal they all wanted to come at once. The Queen appealed emotionally to General Grey for mercy:

> The Queen is terrified at the amount of people (from a mistaken idea of convenience) who are coming to-day, nothing tires the Queen more than that.

'The new ones' – the Gladstone Cabinet of 1868

Rather <u>several</u> days than <u>one long one</u>. It is not the least necessary to bring everything before the Queen goes to Osborne. The Officers of State could kiss hands on <u>Saturday</u> without any Council & the Queen could <u>easily</u> have a Council on the 21st or 22nd at Osborne for <u>any</u> other appointments which require it, or to receive any other people who had to receive <u>white</u> Wands. The Queen dreads today's work <u>very</u> much. <u>Quite</u> alone; not <u>one</u> of her Sons even by her side! General Grey will feel for her. Time does not make this <u>less painful</u>.[145]

The painfulness was to plague the Queen for some years yet. It occasioned even more serious Parliamentary and press criticism than in 1868 and led not only to renewed talk of abdication, but to republican sentiments being expressed in the House of Commons. These ceased after 1872 as the country rallied in support of the monarchy and as the Queen came to terms with her condition and the painfulness faded.

The Queen found it difficult to warm to Gladstone. Almost a year after he became Prime Minister she commented tersely to Princess Victoria: 'I cannot find him very agreeable. He talks so very much. He looks dreadfully ill.'

So Queen Victoria's holiday in Switzerland was only an interlude. But without this respite, an eventful and anxious year might have become an intolerable one for her, with dramatic consequences.

As for the Queen's own health, even her now firmer, clearer handwriting showed that her physical condition and state of mind had certainly taken a turn for the better as a result of her stay in Lucerne – although, as usual, the Queen was the last to admit that Switzerland had done her nerves good. In some of her references to Switzerland there are words such as 'relaxing'[146] and 'southern climate'[147]; that difficult mid-August week – without bracing air – had definitely left its mark.

But so had the more positive aspects of her stay. Towards the end of it she had told Lord Stanley that she was much pleased with Switzerland and was contemplating coming again another year.[148] And on the journey back to England she wrote to Princess Victoria:'I am sorry that our pleasant quiet visit to that splendid country Switzerland is over – which was so very successful – without one single contretemps and without one single entirely bad day! And yet I am glad to go home. We were never kept in once.'[149]

THE RIGHT HON. W. E. GLADSTONE.

Hardly had she arrived at Balmoral a few days later than the Queen was complaining about the weather they were having in Scotland – a belated tribute to the Swiss weather, showing that she remembered more than the Föhn and its ravages: *A dull, raw, chilly day, rather a trying contrast after the great heat, – & cloudless sky we had so long.*[150]

Next day she thought of Switzerland again: *… drive in the Balloch Bhui … No sun shone, but the country looked fine, wild and peculiar, when one does not try to compare it with the immense height of the Swiss mountains, or the marvellous forms of that ideal country.*[151]

In Lucerne the Queen had commissioned paintings from the well-known Swiss landscape artist J.J. Zelger, to whom she had been recommended by the German artist F.X. Winterhalter, portraitist of royalty. Two are reproduced on pp. 67 & 109. Of the six large oil paintings (at Sfrs. 1,000 each) and two watercolours (at Sfrs. 100), no less than three oils were to depict the view from the Pension Wallis – in the morning, at noon and in the evening. When the pictures arrived in England (in good time for Christmas) the Queen returned one of them because she found the sky 'so unfriendly'.[152] An amended painting was accordingly sent to the Queen, to her full satisfaction.

In the months and years to come, as she travelled around her realm and other countries, Queen Victoria was to note down many a resemblance or

Queen Victoria's reminder of Switzerland on the Balmoral Sociable (now at the Royal Mews, Buckingham Palace)

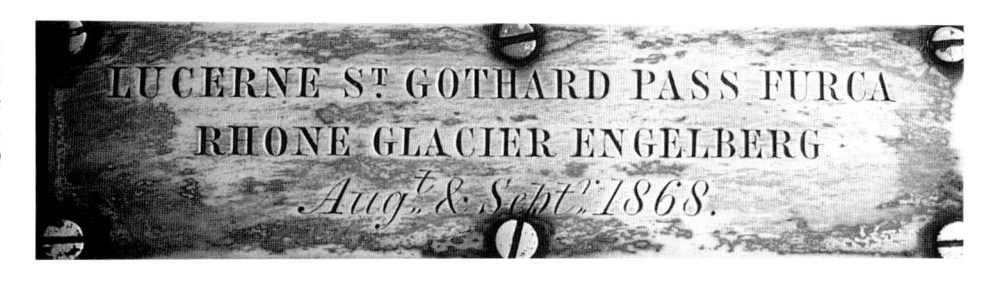

contrast to what she was seeing and what she vividly remembered of her weeks in Switzerland – a lake here, a valley or a mountain contour there. Recording a trip in Scotland a year after her Swiss visit, she noted in her Journal that *we at once got into our celebrated sociable, which has been to the top of the Furca in Switzerland*.[153] In fact, she had an ever-present reminder of Switzerland engraved on a plaque and placed on the back of the box, so that facing her as she sat in the sociable driving around in the Highlands she could see the names of some of the Swiss places to which she had been in it. Nor did she fail to add a footnote to a Journal entry about riding her pony Sultan: *I rode him up to the top of the Righi (nr Lucerne) … in 1868.*[154]

And in 1879, when staying in Italy at Baveno on Lake Maggiore (the northern shores of which are in Switzerland), she rounded off an account of a boat trip by writing in her Journal: *We had a delightful expedition, which reminded me of our pleasant Swiss excursions, & I only wish I had more such.*[155]

Queen Victoria never returned to Switzerland, although she twice passed through by train on her way from France to Germany (in 1885 and 1890). Both occasions were duly recorded in her Journal.

Locarno, as the Queen would have seen it on her last excursion on Lago Maggiore

1885
April 22
... Our first stop was at Bellegarde, on the Swiss frontier, & then on to Geneva, before reaching which we suddenly saw Mont Blanc, quite without a cloud, rising above the town & the other mountains in its spotless whiteness. Emily Peel* with her son & 3 younger daughters was at the station, & they gave me beautiful nosegays. Directly after leaving Geneva, we came upon the Lake, which is very broad & almost like the Solent. The shores at this end, are very flat, but we soon saw Mont Blanc again, this giant, with its surrounding peaks. The afternoon was brilliantly fine, & frightfully hot. Made a short stop at Nyon, & also at Lausanne. All the fruit & chestnut trees were covered with blossom, which had a lovely effect with the snow mountains in the background. By degrees the light faded away & the mountains stood boldly out against the crimson sky. It was a glorious sight. I do so admire the beauties of Switzerland, & was so glad to get this glimpse of it again after 17 years. It was quite dark when we got to Fribourg, where we waited about 2 hours, & had dinner. It had grown a little cooler, which was a great relief.

Five years later to the day Queen Victoria was once more on her way through Switzerland on the same route, again without setting foot on Swiss soil. But this time she was given a rousing reception at Lausanne.

1890
April 22
... By the time we reached Geneva it was raining heavily. Mr. Barton & a Deputation of the English were at the station, & presented me with an address, & Ly.Emily & her daughter Mrs. Barton (my godchild) gave us beautiful flowers. After leaving we took some tea. Alas! the beautiful mountains & Mont Blanc I had so much enjoyed seeing 5 years ago, were not to be distinguished, & we might as well have been in Holland, as in Switzerland. By the time we reached Lausanne it was quite dark. There another Deputation presented me with an address, & a sweet little 3 year old girl, daughter of the British Vice Consul, gave me a bouquet. A Band played & the station was decorated with Chinese lanterns. We had some dinner, & after it, Beatrice stepped out & brought in Alphonse Mensdorff's 2nd daughter Sophie Kinsky,† with her 3 daughters & only son.... They remained about 10 minutes & then left. There were great crowds, who cheered, & sang 'God save the Queen'.

* Lady Emily Peel, daughter of the eighth Marquess of Tweeddale. One of her daughters, Victoria, married Daniel F.P. Barton who was to become British Consul in Geneva.
† Queen Victoria's cousin once removed.

On another occasion Queen Victoria passed through Switzerland en route between Italy and Germany, stopping at Lucerne, where she saw the stalwart guide Antoine Hofmann, who had done so much to provide her with varied and successful expeditions in 1868. Alleged sightings of the Queen at other times and in other parts of Switzerland were reported, but resulted from the presence at various times of a variety of Empresses, Queens and Princesses named Victoria, the name being confusingly popular in royal and aristocratic families. There were also legends, the most persistent of which – firmly anchored in French-Swiss folklore – tells of Queen Victoria having been given an islet off the southeastern shore of the Lake of Geneva and having returned it smartly to its Swiss donors when they served a tax demand (a disgraceful insinuation). Diligent searches have been made in many an archive, but none have yielded a shred of evidence.

On her many further travels abroad, the Queen continued to use the device of travelling incognita, which had served her so well in Switzerland. But 'Countess of Kent' was no longer available after 1874, when the Duke of Edinburgh, her son Prince Alfred, married. Since the title Earl of Kent was one of his, she had been free to use it as long as he was unmarried. But his wife now became Countess of Kent as well as Duchess of Edinburgh – and going abroad as her own daughter-in-law was not the Queen's idea of fun. For her first visit to Italy in 1879 she chose the name 'Countess of Balmoral', and she continued to use this name on her increasingly frequent visits to Italy and France.

But with the passing of time the effect wore off, so that on her later appearances in France in the 1890s she was given royal welcomes by enthusiastic crowds and treated as Queen by the authorities. Colonel Ponsonby's son, the later Sir Frederick Ponsonby was a member of the Queen's Court accompanying her on her visits to France in the 1890s. His memoirs contain an account of one of these, starting with the Queen's arrival in France after crossing the Channel.

> On the pier was a beautiful red velvet and gold lace tent for her to sit in, with a guard of honour of the French Army, while a host of Generals, Admirals and officials hoping to be presented were drawn up near the tent. What with the band playing and the crowd continually cheering vociferously, it was difficult to hear anything ... we travelled comfortably by train across France ... At Nice the whole town turned out and lined the streets from the station to the hotel. There were four regiments of infantry and a battery of artillery to keep back the ever enthusiastic crowd. At the station the Préfect, the Mayor, the General and a host of men in evening clothes and tall hats were assembled.[156]

By this time, though, the Queen could accept such formalities on her journeys abroad. Incognito had done its work.

Axenstein. The pavilion marking the spot where the Queen admired the view on 8 September 1868

10   Echo in Switzerland

Queen Victoria's visit in 1868 echoed far and wide throughout the land. For the Swiss, this was the visit that launched a ship – and much else besides. The new steamship *Victoria* started plying the Lake of Lucerne in 1871, while all over Switzerland hotels called 'Victoria' were mushrooming. The fashion for English-sounding names had started before the Queen's visit, but her presence accelerated it. Astute hoteliers were well aware of the pulling-power of this name. One hotel did not even have to change its name to mark its connection, because it was the only hotel (apart from the Pension Wallis) in which the Queen herself had stayed – the inn on the Furka. For the hymn-writer Frances Ridley Havergal a stay there in 1871 was worth writing home about: 'The Inn here was very small, but is being enlarged. We have a very comfortable little room with a table and sofa, and are royally lodged, for here the Queen slept when she was in Switzerland, in this very room! Hitherto, being the only English we have been taken into the best rooms at once.'[157]

The Queen's visit to Hertenstein on the Lake of Lucerne on 3 September 1868 is commemorated by a memorial stone with a Latin inscription set in the

The steamship *Victoria* on the lake of Lucerne

Stone inscription at Hertenstein, where Queen Victoria walked in September 1868

highest point of the grounds where the Queen walked. The spot is called 'Victoria Hill' and, sure enough, a hotel was established nearby.

Not only hotels played on the Queen's name and its connotations. When the British Consul in Geneva sponsored a new concert hall there in the 1890s it was, of course, named Victoria Hall.

The Queen's Diamond Jubilee in 1897 was celebrated in Switzerland not only by the considerable British colony but with the active participation of large numbers of Swiss – and the Swiss press noted especially that the British flag was flying from the Pension Wallis.

There were whole columns about the celebrations taking place in the British Isles and Empire, emphasizing the enormous popularity and loyalty the Queen enjoyed (to say nothing of her enormous family: nine children, forty grandchildren and thirty great-grandchildren, making a grand total of seventy-nine direct descendants). Erudite articles dwelt on the depth and strength of Anglo-Swiss relations, for example recalling with gratitude how swift British diplomatic action had saved the Swiss Confederation at its birth in 1848 from interventionist

Goblet presented by Queen Elizabeth I in 1560 to the Zurich reformer H. Bullinger

threats on the part of its neighbours. During a glittering reception in Zürich the British Consul-General handed around a silver and gold goblet (filled for the occasion with wine) which had been presented in 1560 by Queen Elizabeth I to the reformer Zwingli's successor Bullinger, in recognition of the way Zürich had harboured English and Scottish Protestants exiled by the Counter-Reformation. Two years later the new English Church of St Mark's at Lucerne was consecrated and it did not pass notice that the Queen had contributed to Anglican church funds at the end of her visit.

In 1968 the centenary of the Queen's visit was marked in Lucerne by a commemorative exhibition in the Swiss Transport Museum there, with the Balmoral Sociable, lent for the summer by H.M. Queen Elizabeth II, as its

Commemorative tablet unveiled in 1968 on the Gütsch, near the former Pension Wallis

centrepiece. At a simple ceremony the Mayor of Lucerne and the British Ambassador to Switzerland unveiled a memorial tablet on the Gütsch near the Pension Wallis (the house still stands but is now divided into apartments).

All this because, in 1868, the Queen of England took another name and escaped to a haven on a hill in a small country where she found not only breathtaking scenery but also the complete change and repose and above all the simple family life she had been vainly seeking for many a tormented year.

References

Abbreviations used:
RA   Royal Archives
PRO   Public Record Office
HHS   Hessische Hausstiftung
Disraeli MSS   Hughenden Papers, Bodleian Library

The source for all quotations from Queen Victoria's Journal is the transcript (made by her youngest daughter, Princess Beatrice) which is in the Royal Archives, with the exception of a few extracts which are taken from printed sources as indicated below.

1 RA, Queen Victoria, Journal, 31 August 1868
2 '*Lord M*', David Cecil (Constable, 1954)
3 Grey Papers, Durham, 25 January 1863
4 Grey Papers, Durham, 5 February 1863
5 Grey Papers, Durham, 4 September 1863
6 Grey Papers, Durham, 28 August 1865
7 Grey Papers, Durham, 29 August 1865
8 Grey Papers, Durham; 29 August 1865
9 Grey Papers, Durham, 30 August 1865
10 Grey Papers, Durham, 1 September 1865
11 *Early Years of the Prince Consort*, C. Grey (London, 1867) pp.154-5
12 Grey Papers, Durham, 17 December 1863, Viscount George Byng Torrington to General Grey (Queen Victoria file 4)
13 Grey Papers, Durham, 4 September 1866
14 Grey Papers, Durham, 5 September 1866
15 Queen Victoria to Lord Russell, 22 January 1866; from *Queen Victoria in her Letters & Journals*, sel. Christopher Hibbert (John Murray,1984) p.192
16 RA, Queen Victoria, Journal, 6 February 1866
17 Grey Papers, Durham, 13 June 1867
18 Grey Papers, Durham, 14 June 1867
19 RA, Add A/15/1103, Major Elphinstone to Queen Victoria, 11 August 1867
20 RA, Queen Victoria, Journal, 4 August 1867
21 RA, Add A25/204, 27–8 August 1867
22 RA, Add A25/205, 6 September 1867
23 RA, Add A15/1137, 25 October 1867
24 Ibid.
25 Grey Papers, Durham, 29 January 1868
26 Grey Papers, Durham, 2 February 1868

27 Disraeli MSS, Bodleian, 6 May 1868
28 Disraeli to Queen Victoria, 12 May 1868, *Letters of Queen Victoria*, 2nd series, vol. 1, ed. Buckle (Murray, 1926)
29 Disraeli MSS, Bodleian B/XIX/A/48, 14 May 1868
30 Queen Victoria to Mr Theodore Martin, 14 May 1868; *Letters of Queen Victoria*, 2nd series, vol. 1, ed. Buckle (John Murray, 1926)
31 Grey Papers, Durham, 22 May 1868
32 Disraeli MSS, Bodleian, B/XIX/A/52, 22 May 1868
33 *Idem*
34 Grey Papers, Durham, 26 May 1868
35 Queen Victoria to Princess Victoria, HHS, 26 May 1868
36 Crown Princess Victoria to Queen Victoria, 2 June 1868, from *Your Dear Letter*, ed. R. Fulford (Evans Brothers Ltd, 1971) p.195
37 Queen Victoria to Princess Victoria, 8 June 1868, from *Your Dear Letter*, ed. R. Fulford (Evans Brothers Ltd, 1971) p.195
38 Queen Victoria to Princess Victoria, HHS, 15 June 1868
39 Queen Victoria to Princess Victoria, HHS, 20 June 1868
40 RA, Queen Victoria, Journal, 22 June 1868
41 Ibid.
42 Queen Victoria to Crown Princess Victoria, HHS, 25 October 1867
43 *Early Years of the Prince Consort*, C. Grey (London, 1867), pp.154-5
44 *The Queen thanks Sir Howard*, M.H. McClintock (John Murray, 1945) p. 107
45 Grey Papers, Durham, 24 March 1868
46 Disraeli MSS, Bodleian B/XX/Ca/28a, 8 April 1868
47 Crown Princess to Queen Victoria, 2 June 1868, from *Your Dear Letter*, ed. R. Fulford (Evans Brothers Ltd, 1971) p.195
48 Queen Victoria to Crown Princess Victoria, HHS, 8 June 1868
49 Politisches Archiv des Auswärtigen Amtes, Bonn, Dépêche No. 115, 30 May 1968
50 Queen Victoria to Crown Princess Victoria, HHS, 15 June 1868
51 Disraeli MSS, Bodleian, B/XIX/D/62, 1 July 1868
52 Disraeli MSS, Bodleian, B/XX/Ca/39, 5 July 1868
53 Queen Victoria, Journal, 7 July 1868
54 Disraeli MSS, Bodleian, B/XIX/D/66, (undated) July 1868
55 Derby Papers, Liverpool, Disraeli to Stanley, 31 July 1868
56 Derby Papers, Liverpool, Diary, 17 June 1868
57 Derby Papers, Liverpool, Diary, 2 July 1868
58 PRO, FO 100/165, No. 43 (Draft), 30 July 1868
59 PRO, FO 192/57, No. 43, 30 July 1868
60 Ibid.
61 PRO, FO 100/170, 27 July 1868
62 RA, Queen Victoria, Journal, 10 September 1873
63 Queen Victoria to Crown Princess Victoria, HHS, 6 July 1868
64 Queen Victoria to Crown Princess Victoria, HHS, 15 July 1868
65 Queen Victoria to Crown Princess Victoria, HHS, 8 July 1868
66 Queen Victoria to Crown Princess Victoria, HHS, 10 July 1868
67 Crown Princess Victoria to Queen Victoria, HHS, 7 July 1868
68 Queen Victoria to Crown Princess Victoria, HHS, 10 July 1868
69 Queen Victoria to Crown Princess Victoria, HHS 29 July 1868
70 Queen Victoria to Crown Princess Victoria, HHS, 1 August 1868

71 Queen Victoria to Crown Princess Victoria, HHS, 22 July 1868
72 RA Add. A25/232, 25 July 1868
73 RA Add. A25/232, 4 August 1868
74 Queen Victoria to Crown Princess Victoria, HHS, 25 July 1868
75 RA Add. A/36/27, 5 August 1868
76 Derby Papers, Liverpool, letter to Lord Lyons, 25 July 1868
77 Derby Papers, Liverpool, Diary, 6 August 1868
78 Disraeli MSS, Bodleian, B/XIX/A/90, 7 August 1868
79 Derby Papers, Liverpool, Diary, 8 August 1868
80 Disraeli MSS, Bodleian, B/XIX/A/82, 7 August 1868
81 Ibid.
82 Queen Victoria to Crown Princess Victoria, HHS, 8 August 1868
83 RA, Queen Victoria, Journal, 8 August 1868
84 The Note-Books of Samuel Butler (A.C. Fifield, London, 1919), p.342
85 RA, Queen Victoria, Journal, 10 August 1868
86 Queen Victoria to Crown Princess Victoria, HHS, 12 August 1868
87 RA, Add A36/28
88 PRO LC 11/194, for Quarter to 30 September 1868
89 Disraeli MSS, Bodleian, B/XIX/D/83, 13 August 1868
90 Derby Papers, Liverpool, Diary, *passim*
91 Derby Papers, Liverpool, Diary, 9 August 1868
92 Queen Victoria, Letters and Journal, *passim*
93 RA, Queen Victoria, Journal, 6 August 1868
94 RA, Queen Victoria, Journal, 7 August 1868
95 Queen Victoria to Crown Princess Victoria, HHS, 15 August 1868
96 Derby Papers, Liverpool, Diary, 16 August 1868
97 Disraeli MSS, Bodleian, B/XIX/A/93, 20 August 1868
98 Queen Victoria to Crown Princess Victoria, HHS, 19 August 1868
99 Disraeli MSS, Bodleian, B/XIX/A/83, 17 August 1868
100 Queen Victoria, Journal, 17 August 1868
101 Disraeli MSS, Bodleian, B/XIX/A/83, 17 August 1868
102 PRO 192/58, 21 August 1868
103 Queen Victoria to Crown Princess Victoria, HHS, 19 August 1868
104 Disraeli MSS, Bodleian, B/XIX/A/94, 23 August 1868
105 RA Add A36/29, 24 August 1868
106 Queen Victoria to Crown Princess Victoria, 30 August 1868, from *Your Dear Letter*, ed. R. Fulford (Evans Brothers Ltd, 1971) p.206
107 RA, Queen Victoria, Journal, 30 August 1868
108 Derby Papers, Liverpool, Diary, 15 August 1868
109 Disraeli MSS, Bodleian, B/XIX/A/86, 31 August 1868
110 Derby Papers, Liverpool, Diary, 1 September 1868
111 Derby Papers, Liverpool, to Lord Lyons, 1 September 1868
112 Disraeli MSS, Bodleian, B/XIX/A/96, 2 September 1868
113 Derby Papers, Liverpool, Diary, 1 September 1868
114 Disraeli MSS, Bodleian, B/XIX/A/96, 2 September 1868
115 RA, Queen Victoria, Journal, 1 September 1868
116 PRO FO 100/170, 14 July 1868
117 Derby Papers, Liverpool, to Disraeli, 29 August 1868
118 PRO, FO 192/59, 12 June 1868
119 RA, Queen Victoria, Journal, 2 September 1868

120 RA, Add. A 36/30, 3 September 1868
121 Queen Victoria to Crown Princess Victoria, HHS, 6 September 1868
122 Derby Papers, Liverpool, 3 September 1868; B24, 128
123 Diary, Derby Papers, Liverpool, 4 September 1868
124 Disraeli MSS, Bodleian, B/XIX/A/98, 5 September 1868
125 Ibid.
126 From Queen Victoria to Crown Princess Victoria, HHS, 3 September 1868
127 Queen Victoria to Crown Princess Victoria, HHS, 6 September 1868
128 Disraeli MSS, Bodleian, B/XIX/A/88, 7 September 1868
129 RA, Add. A 36/30, 3 September 1868
130 Queen Victoria to Crown Princess Victoria, HHS, 6 September 1868
131 Queen Victoria to Crown Princess Victoria, HHS, 10 September 1868
132 RA, Queen Victoria, Journal, 10 September 1868
133 Disraeli MSS, Bodleian, B/XIX/A/89, 10 September 1868
134 RA, Queen Victoria, Journal, 10 September 1868
135 *The Times*, 14 September 1868
136 RA A37/51, Disraeli to Queen Victoria, 10 September 1868
137 Ibid.
138 RA, A 37/50, 31 August 1868
139 *The Times*, 15 September 1868
140 Disraeli MSS, Bodleian B/XIX/A/76, 3 September 1868
141 Disraeli MSS, Bodleian B/XIX/A/77, 3 September 1868
142 Disraeli MSS, Bodleian B/XIX/D/69
143 RA, Queen Victoria, Journal, 23 November 1868
144 Grey Papers, Durham, 23 November 1868
145 Grey Papers, Durham, 9 December 1868
146 Grey Papers, Durham, 23 December 1868
147 Queen Victoria to Crown Princess Victoria, HHS, 6 September 1893
148 Derby Papers, Liverpool, 23 December 1868
149 Queen Victoria to Crown Princess Victoria, 10 September 1868
150 RA, Queen Victoria, Journal, 16 September 1868
151 RA, Queen Victoria, Journal, 17 September 1868
152 Zelger family papers 302, 303; R Löhlein to J.J. Zelger 10 December 1868 and 2 January 1869
153 RA, Queen Victoria, 1 September 1869 (in *More Leaves from our Life in the Highlands*)
154 RA, Queen Victoria, 4 September 1869 (in *More Leaves from our Life in the Highlands*)
155 RA, Queen Victoria, Journal, 17 April 1879
156 *Recollections of Three Reigns*, Sir Frederick Ponsonby (Eyre & Spottiswoode, 1951), p.53
157 F.R. Havergal, *Swiss Letters and Alpine Poems* (J. Nisbet, London, 1881), 3 July 1871, p.131

Illustration Sources

Abbreviations used:
RA   Royal Archives, Windsor Castle
RL   Royal Library, Windsor Castle
ZL   Zentralbibliothek Luzern (Lucerne Central Library)
NPG   National Portrait Gallery, London
PRO   Public Record Office

p.15 RA
p.17 Ibid.
p.18 Photograph: RA. Quotation by courtesy of Hessische Hausstiftung, Fulda
p.21 By courtesy of M. Auturo Hofmann
p.23 By courtesy of NPG, London
p.27 RA
p.28 By courtesy of NPG, London
p.31 RA
p.32 Disraeli MMS, Bodleian, B/XIX/A/52, 22 May 1868. By permission of Bodley's Librarian and the National Trust
p.33 RA
p.37 Ibid.
p.41 ZL, LSc: 3:9
p.44 RA
p.45 Public Record Office, FO 100/165, 30 July 1868. By permission of PRO
p.47 Imperial Calendar 1868 pp.88–9. By permission of the British Library BS 40/22
p.48 RA
p.51 Roger-Viollet Archive, Paris
p.58–9 RA
p.60 Ibid.
p.62 Sketch map by R.C.F. Eden, MBE, Berne
p.63 Roger-Viollet Archive, Paris
p.64 By courtesy of Swiss Transport Museum, Lucerne
p.65 Photograph: RA. Quotation by courtesy of Hessische Hausstiftung, Fulda
p.66 ZL, LSc: 10:9:2
p.67 By courtesy of Professor F. Zelger, Zurich
p.68 RL, K 42, f16c
p.69 RL, K 725
p.71 *top left & right* ZL, LSc: 4:18
p.71 *bottom* Archive Josef Gwerder, Meggen
p.72 ZL, URb: 20:10:32
p.73 ZL, URb: 5:1:1
p.74 *left* By courtesy of Stadtarchiv Luzern (Lucerne Municipal Archive)
p.74 *right* RL, K 736
p.75 ZL, LSb: 5:6:5
p.79 RL, K 42, f9c
p.80 ZL, SZb: 6:22:9
p.81 ZL, SZc: 1:43:8
p.82 RL, K 786
p.84 Sketch map by R.C.F. Eden, MBE, Berne

p.85 *left* ZL, URb: 9:1:7
p.85 *right* ZL, URc: 7:2:3
p.86 ZL, URb: 24:1:2
p.87 ZL, URc: 3:12:2
pp.88–9 RL, K 708
p.93 RL, K 42, f13
p.94 RL, K 704
p.95 RL, K 42, f11b
p.96 RL, K 42, f12
p.97 RL, K 42, f14v
p.100 RL, K 709
p.102 ZL, RIb: 1:2:5
p.103 ZL, RIb: 2:3:6
pp.104–5 *top* ZL, RIc: 1:8:1
p.104 *bottom* RL, K 42, f16a
p.106 *top left* ZL, NWc: 11:5:1
p.106 *top right* ZL, NWb: 11:4:2
p.106 *bottom* RL, K 42, f17
p.107 By courtesy of the Abbot of Engelberg
p.109 By courtesy of Frau M.M. Freuler-Bühler, Basel
p.110 RA
p.114 RL, K 42, f27
p.115 RL, K 42, f21c
p.119 By courtesy of M. Arturo Hofmann
p.120 RL, K 42, f21b
p.122 ZL, URb: 18:1:2
p.123 *top* ZL, 4119–9
p.123 *bottom* RL, K 42, f25b
p.124 RL, K 42, f23b
p.127 RL, K 742
p.128 RL, K 42, f25a
p.142 Private Collection. Photograph: Courtauld Institute of Art
p.145 By courtesy of NPG, London
p.146 Ibid.
p.147 *top* RA, BP 20131
p.147 *bottom* By courtesy of Mr Peter Barber, British Library
p.150 From *'Poesien und Bilder von Axenstein'* (J.A. Preuss, Zurich). ZL (Bürgerbibliothek, Bro. 8°)
p.151 Swiss Transport Museum
p.152 *top* Photograph by Franziska Amstad Betschart
p.152 *bottom* By courtesy of Swiss Natioal Museum, Zurich
p.153 Photograph by Emanuel Ammon

Index

Entries in italic type refer to illustrations

abdication, 16, 31–2, 145
Abyssinia, 27
Albert, Prince Consort, *15*, 15–17, 18–20, 24, 27, 29, 37, 50, 54, 60, 66, 101, 129–31
Alexander II, Czar, 142
Alfred, Prince, Duke of Edinburgh (second son of Queen Victoria), 8, 27, 43, 142–3, 149
Alice, Princess (second daughter of Queen Victoria), 18, 50
Alpnach, 98, 108
Amsteg, 86, 98
Arolla, 70
Arthur, Prince (third son of Queen Victoria), 19–20, *21*, 24, 37, *58*, 60, 98, 101, 103, 108
Austria, 18–20, 24, 37, 53, 118
Axenstein, 129, *150*
Axenstrasse, 72, *73*, 129

Balmoral Castle, 17, 27, 30–1, *31*, 33, 40, 78, 128, 134, 140–1, 146
Barton, Daniel F.P. (British Consul, Geneva), 148, 152
Basle, 56, 63, 65, 78, 118
Bauer, Fräulein (Governess to Princess Beatrice), 50, *59*, 73, 98, 121, 130
Baveno, Italy, 147
Beatrice, Princess (fifth daughter of Queen Victoria), 8, 11, *58*, 59, 64, 82, 84, 93, 98, 112, 121, 128, 140–1, 148
Beer, Swiss, 118–20
Belgium, 112, 117, 143–4
Benz (coachman), 108, 111, 128–9
Bernstorff, Count Albrecht von, 40
Biddulph, Lady Mary (Hon. Bedchamber Woman), 50, *58*, 66, 73, 82, 98, 113, 121, 128
Biddulph, Sir Thomas (Keeper of the Privy Purse), 8, 50, *59*, 66, 68, 71, 73–4, 74, 76, 83, 85–6, 96, 98–9, 112, 117, 119, 121, 141–2
Birs, 63
Bismarck, Otto von, 143
Brassey, Thomas, 64
Bremble, John de, 87
Brown, Archie, 47, 60, 81
Brown, John, 38, 47, 60, 65, 67, 74, 81, 86, 92, 94–5, 107, 110, *110*, 120, 128
Brünig Pass, 121–2
Brunnen, 72–3, 80, 129
Buckingham Palace, 15, 28, 34, 75, 117, 147
Bullinger, H. (Zürich Reformer), 152–3
Bund, Der, 47, 90–1
Butler, Samuel, 70

Cairns, Lord Chancellor, 38, 43, 113
Canterbury, Archbishop of, 143
Cecil, David, 16
Cham, 81
Charlotte, Empress of Mexico, 117
Cherbourg, 51, 56, 131–2
Churches, British, in Switzerland, 70, 153
Church of England, 27, 68, 70, 84, 99, 107, 113–15, 124, 140–1, 143
Coburg, 17–19, 42–3

Darmstadt, 18–20, 53, 125, 142
Derby, 14th Earl of (Prime Minister), 25–6
Devil's Bridge, 87, *87*, 90, 97
Disraeli, Benjamin (Prime Minister), 7, 26–30, 27, 32–4, 42–4, 54, 67, 76, 80, 82, 84, 92, 112–14, 124–6, 130, 139, *142*, 140–4
Dowager Queen Elisabeth of Prussia, 124–6, 129–30, 132
Duckworth, Revd J.R. (Governor to Prince Leopold), 50, *58*, 69, 73, 81, 98, 107–8, 124, 127

Elphinstone, Howard, Governor to Prince Arthur, 19, 24–5, *37*, 37–8, 49, 60, 98
Ely, Jane, Marchioness of, 8, 50–1, *59*, 67–8, 71, 73, 81–2, 92–5, 98, 101, 104, 107–8, 110, 112–13, 121–2, 124–8, 130
Emmental, 70
Engelberg, 80, 86, 104–5, *106*, 107–8, 120, 124, 134
Eugénie, Empress of France, 51–5, 112–13, 124–6, 132–3, 142

Fenians, 27, 52, 84, 98–9
Flanders, Count of, 117
Flora (one of the Queen's ponies), 70, 108, 110, *110*, 122
Flüelen, 72–3, 85–6, *85*, 90, 98, 110
Föhn, 78, 80, 146
France, 39, 51–3, 112–13, 130, 132, 143–4, 147, 149
Fribourg, 148
Furka Pass, 82, 84–5, *88–9*, 90, 92, 93, *94*, *95*, 97–9, 101, 118, 134, 140, 147, 151

General Election, 25, 27, 42, 80, 99, 113, 115, 126, 141, 144
Geneva, 46, 134, 148–9, 152
Giswyl, 122
Gladstone, W.E., Liberal Leader, then Prime Minister, 27–8, 142, *142*, 144–5, *145*, *146*
Globe and Traveller, The, 28–9, 30, 44
Goldau, 81, *81*, 103
Göschenen, 86, 90, 98
Grey, General Charles, Private Secretary to Queen Victoria, 7, 16–24, *17*, 26–7, 32–3, 38, 42–3, 143–5
Grindelwald, 49, 134
Gütsch, 41, 67, 153, *153*

Hauenstein Tunnel (upper), 63–4, *64*
Havergal, Frances Ridley, 151
Helena, Princess (third daughter of Queen Victoria), 23, 99
Helps, Arthur (Clerk of the Privy Council), 30, 140
Hergiswil, 111
Herrgotteswald, *127*, 127–8
Hertenstein, 121, 151–2, *152*
Highlands of Scotland, 19, 25, 29–30, 38, 47, 57, 60, 80, 86, 90, 97, 121, 128, 133, 141, 147
Hodgins, J.G., 60
Hofmann, Antoine (guide), *21*, 60, 65, 67, 71, 86, 92, 94–7, 102, 105, 110, 112,

119, 122, 129–30, 149
Honolulu, Queen Emma of, 22
Hospenthal, 90, 97

incognito, 36, 40, 42–5, 52–3, 57, 65, 82, 116–18, 124, 131–2, 149
Italy, 70, 147, 149

Jenner, Sir William, Physician to Queen Victoria, 24, 32, 38, 40, 44, 50, 54, *59*, 67, 74–5, 80, 85–6, 98, 121

Kaiserstuhl, 122
Kanné, J.J. (Queen Victoria's Director of Continental journeys), 19, 49–50, 60, 65, 74, 82, 84, 90, 92
Kent, Countess of (Queen Victoria when incognita), 15, 36, 43, 45, 49, 53, 57, 90, 107, 139, 149
Klimserhorn, 111
Kriens, 69, 104

Latrobe, J.H.B., 92
Lausanne, 148
Legation, British, in Berne 42, 45–6, 76, 83, 118–19
Leopold, Prince (fourth son of Queen Victoria), 41, *58*, 73, 81, 98, 107, 127, 132, 140–1
Lion Monument, *75*, 75–6
Louise, Princess (fourth daughter of Queen Victoria), 7, 23, 32, 49, 51, *58*, *69*, 71, 73–4, *74*, 81, *82*, 85, *88*–9, 90, 92–3, *94*, 94–6, 98, *100*, 104, 107–8, 110, 113, 121, 124, *127*, 127–32, 140–1
Lowertz, lake, *80*, 81, 103
Lucerne, 25, 40–1, *41*, 42, 45–7, 49–51, 53, 56, 58, 63, 65–7, *67*, 69, 70, 72, *75*, 75–7, 83, 92, 97–8, 112, 114, 116–17, 119, 121, 124–7, 129–34, 139–40, 146, 149, 153
Lucerne, lake of, 37, 41, *41*, 56–7, *62*, 65–6, *67*, *68*, 69, *69*, 70, *71*, 72, *72*, 73, *73*, 85, *85*, 98, *100*, 101–3, 105, 109–11, *114*, 115, *115*, 118, *120*, 121–4, 129, 134, 151, *151*
Lumley, John Savile (H.M. Minister to Switzerland), 42, 45, 46, 76–7, 83–4
Lungern, Lake of, 98, 122
Lyons, Lord, H.M. Ambassador to France, 51–5, 112–13, 130–2

McNeile, Hugh, appointed Dean of Ripon, 99
Maggiore, Lake, 147, *147*
Marie, Grand Duchess (daughter of Czar Alexander II), 142–3
Martin, Theodore, 29–30
Morschach, 129
Muttenhorn, 93

Napoleon III, Emperor of France, 44, 51–3, 63, 113, 126, 130–1
Neuchâtel conflict (1856–7), 64

Olten, 11, 65
Osborne House, 34, 44, 47–8, *48*, 50, 134, 145

Paris, 44, 46, 51–4, 56, 68, 78, 112–13, 124–6, 130–2, 139, 144–5
Parliament, 22–3, *23*, 25, 27, 28, 30–1, 33–4, 38–40, 45, 76, 116, 140, 144–5
Peel, Lady Emily, 148
Pfaffensprung, 98
Phipps, Sir Charles, 18
Pilatus, 57, 67, 69, 73, 108–13, *109*, *115*, 116, 123–4, 127, 129, 134
Ponsonby, Henry, Equerry to Queen Victoria, 50–1, *59*, 66–8, 73–4, 81, 98–9, 101, 107–8, 121–2, 127, 130, 149
Prussia, 7, 20, 33, 40, 53, 64, 68, 112–13, 124–6, 129, 132, 143–4

Realp, 90–1
Reform Bill, Second (1867), 30, 141
republicanism, 90, 118, 145
Reuss, 65, 86
Rhone Glacier, 91–7, *93*, 99, 134, 140
Rigi, 37, 57, 67, 69, 81, 99, 101–5, *102*–4, 109, 111–12, *114*, 121, 134, 147
Riss, 19–20
Rosenau, 19, 40
Rossberg, landslip of, 81
Russell, Earl (Lord John) (Prime Minister), 22
Russia, 53, 142
Rüttimatt, 107

St Cloud, 130
St Gotthard, 49, *84*, 85, 87, 90, 97, 99, 134
Sanderson, T.H. (Private Secretary to Lord Stanley), 111
Sarnen, Lake of, 109, 121
Schleswig-Holstein, Prince and Princess Christian (Helena, q.v.) of, 141

Schwarzenberg, *79*, 127
Schwyzer Mythen, 123, *123*
Seeburg, 82, 103
Seelisberg, 122–3, *122*
Sempach, Lake of, 65, 109
Sissach, 63
sociable, Balmoral, 47, 65, *65*, 93, 108, 147, *147*, 153
Stanley, Lord, Foreign Secretary, 40, 42, *44*, 44–6, 53–4, 68, 76, 80, 82–3, 92, 98, 111–17, 124–5, 140, 143, 146
Stans, 105, *106*
Stansstad, 73, 80, 105, 108
Strachey, Lytton, 16
Sultan (one of the Queen's ponies), 108, 147

Tell's chapel, 71–4, *72,85*, 86
Tell, William, 73–4, 86, 123
Times, The, 23–4, 30, 45, 56, 131, 133, 140
Titlis, 70, 134
Toko of Denmark, 74
Torrington, Viscount, 21
Treib, 122, *122*
Tyrol, 19, 24, 34

Usk, Adam of, 87

Victoria, Crown Princess of Prussia (eldest daughter of Queen Victoria), 7, 18, 33, *33*, 34, 40, 48–9, 65, 68–9, 73, 79–81, 85, 108, 123–6, 128, 130, 145–6
Victoria, Queen,
  photos of, *15, 18, 60, 110*
  pictures by, *68, 79, 93, 95, 96, 97, 104, 106, 114, 115, 120, 124, 128*
  text, passim
Victoria and Albert (Royal yacht), 50–1, 132
Victoria, steamship, 151, *151*
Villiger, Anselm (Abbot of Engelberg), 107–8

Wales, Prince of, 30, 32, 43
Wallis, Pension, 41, 49, 66, *66*, 69, *71*, 73, *74*, 74, 80, 83, 85, 98, 101, 108, 113, 118, 121, 129, 146, 151–3
Wassen, 86, *86*, *97*, 98
Weggis, 73, 101
Wilhelm, Prince, later Emperor of Germany, 108
Windsor, 7, 22, 30, 34, 44, 48, 74, 128, 139–41
Winkelried, Arnold von, *106*
Winkelried, steamer, 70–3, *71*, 80, 85, 98, 101, 106, 108, 118, 122, 128–9
Winterhalter, F.X., 146

Zelger, J.J., *67, 109*, 146
Zug, 81, 103